# Parents, Kids, & Sexual Integrity

BOOKS BY DONALD M. JOY

*Bonding: Relationships in the Image of God*
*Re-Bonding: Preventing and Restoring Damaged Relationships*
*Meaningful Learning in the Church*
*Moral Development Foundations*
*Lovers—Whatever Happened to Eden?* (with Robbie Joy)

# Donald M. Joy, Ph.D.

# Parents, Kids, & Sexual Integrity

## Equipping Your Child for Healthy Relationships

**WORD BOOKS**
PUBLISHER
WACO, TEXAS

A DIVISION OF
WORD, INCORPORATED

**Library of Congress Cataloging in Publication Data:**

Joy, Donald M. (Donald Marvin), 1928–
    Parents, kids & sexual integrity: equipping your child for
healthy relationships/Donald M. Joy.
        p.    cm.
    Includes index.
    1. Sexual ethics—United States.   2. Sexual ethics for
teenagers.   3. Premarital sex—United States.   4. Family—
United States—Religious life.   5. Sex—Religious aspects—
Christianity.   I. Title.   II. Title: Parents, kids, and sexual
integrity.
HQ31.J77 1988
649′ .65—dc19                                             88–151
                                                            CIP

89801239 FG 987654321
*Printed in the United States of America*

For
**Steve and Carol Seamands**
**Matthew**
**Jason**
**Joseph**
**and Stephanie**

whose adventures in family development we admire

# Contents

$\triangle$

# Foreword

△

No one can adequately describe the experience of reading a book in which the mind, heart, and soul of a Christian scholar come together in a bold statement that strikes at the heart of a contemporary issue and speaks to both the Christian and the secular communities. Dr. Donald Joy has achieved that worthy goal in his book, *Parents, Kids, and Sexual Integrity*.

For more than thirty years, Dr. Joy has been a student of family dynamics. His research has made him a noteworthy professor with a great appeal to the students of Asbury Theological Seminary who have a strong desire to learn from him. Yet a reputation for scholarship and teaching is not enough. Many other professors of Christian education, moral development, and family relationships would qualify. Dr. Joy's personal and pastoral experience, however, are the genius of his teaching and writing. Throughout his writing, there are windows of personal experience with which all of us can identify. The depth and breadth of these word pictures form a bridge of credibility between his scholarship and its application to life situations that not only give his writing credibility but cause us to sit up and pay attention.

For example, in preparation for my writing this foreword,

Dr. Joy gave me a copy of his manuscript with the suggestion that I read the introduction and two chapters. Once I started reading, however, I did not stop. Every page has insights that urge you on to the next. *Parents, Kids, and Sexual Integrity* is a model for writing with substance, style, and spirit.

Make no mistake. The spiritual quality of Donald Joy's writing does not mean that he is soft on the nagging issues relating to parents, children, and families. After reading his introduction, I decided that he should be dubbed a "Slayer of Social Myths." Citing his experience as a participant in a conference on teenage pregnancy, he listened impatiently to researchers recite gloomy statistics and social workers propose palliatives for the problem. As a voice in the wilderness, he called the conference from the treatment of teenagers and their tragic symptoms toward the idea of risk proofing them through the systemic roots of the family. If his listeners heard only a rehash of the traditional family and its values, they were wrong.

While Dr. Joy does not apologize for his biblical stance, he is not in the camp of those who apply the letter of the law and its narrow interpretation as the resolution to the problems of the contemporary family. Rather, through careful study of the whole Word of God, the spirit of the law breaks through to us from a larger and more meaningful perspective. The result is one of the most important contributions of the book to the problems confronting the contemporary family, a survey of characteristic family systems. Whether we as readers represent the traditional nuclear family, the rebonded second or third family, or the single-parent family, we will find ourselves in the models and benefit from the recommendations.

Still another myth that the author slays is the idea that nothing has changed in the society which affects the morals and meaning of youth. Earlier pubescence and deferred adulthood without definitive rites of passage is certainly a sound diagnosis for the symptoms from which our youth suffer today. In clear language, he describes the sexual, economic, moral, and spiritual symptoms that fill in the gap between puberty and adulthood. Dr. Joy also dares to say that the reason for the disease is our failure to recognize that times have changed. Our children are caught in the crunch. We will not like the truth he speaks when he blames parents for filling in the gap, not just with the indulgence of money and toys, but with relational incompetence and moral inconsistency. We will see ourselves in his diagnosis, and it will hurt.

Do not get the wrong impression. While Dr. Joy does not spare social workers who treat only symptoms or preachers who give simplistic answers to the mounting problems of parents, children, and families today, he speaks the hard truth with gracious love. A tone of hope permeates the book, even in the chapters that deal so pointedly with our cherished myths. Each chapter, for instance, begins with a parable drawn from either Dr. Joy's family or his lifetime ministry with teenagers and students. The stories are especially meaningful to me because I know that Don and Robbie Joy have made their home the center for an extended family that is tied together with letters, telephone calls, and drop-in visits. Although he downplays his part in counseling and restoring the persons whom he introduces in his book, I can assure you that the patience, wisdom, and grace that you sense in him and his wife are real.

The constructive spirit of *Parents, Kids, and Sexual Integrity* comes to a fitting conclusion in the final chapters of the book with the promise of the intimate family. Of course, it is an ideal that causes conviction, frustration, rebuttal, and hope—all at the same time. Yet I dare say that each of us will come away from the book with a desire to put into effect some of the changes that can make a difference in our families. Never again will a child or grandchild's touch on the arm, tackle from behind, or hug around the neck be the same. Never again will their cries of anger, requests for time, or prayers of love go unheeded. Without creating some new lockstep for parenting, Dr. Joy has sensitized me to the meaning, and especially the joys, of intimacy in relationships with my family. His book will be on the front shelf of my library as one to read again and recommend enthusiastically to scholars and social workers, pastors and parents, adults and kids. Whether our thinking is Christian or secular, whether our families are well or hurting, Donald Joy has given us a book whose meaning is current and whose value is timeless.

DAVID L. MCKENNA
*President*
*Asbury Theological Seminary*
*Wilmore, Kentucky*

# Introduction

$\triangle$

This is a book about family relationships that "risk proof" children and teens against compulsive experimentation and use of alcohol, sex, and drugs. In it I will contend that the gift of sexuality is profoundly at the core of personality and is most vulnerable to damage in the child-rearing years. I will also offer mutual respect and the parental gift of responsibility as keys to "risk proofing" the kids. My thesis is relatively simple: *Our sexuality is profoundly complicated and does not merely consist of organs or sensations or actions or events. It is, instead, the core of our personhood.*

*Because our sexuality is at the center of personality, it is also the "first morality." Thus everything having to do with sexual feelings and behavior is colored either with the ecstasy of "ultimate good" or with the tragedy of "ultimate evil." Simultaneously, this mysterious gift is the source of (1) personal identity, (2) pleasure, (3) reproduction, and (4) the glue of pair-bonding by which two people are almost literally laminated into one body, one mind, one energy, and one vision.*

### Trivializing Sexuality

This is not a report on teen pregnancy rates or on the technology of promiscuity. The current preoccupation with pregnancy prevention and disease control tends to miss the heart of the sexual issue. Safe sex in the face of today's AIDS epidemic trivializes sexual activity and guarantees that today's practices will remain forever outside and apart from the meaning of sexual intimacy and communication. Abortion and pregnancy control suggest that as long as there is no pregnancy—or at least no baby—anything is appropriate to the amoral game of frustrated adolescents who only want to play house on week nights and weekends. Responsible views on fertility and the power of creating new life are withheld. Thus we presuppose (and anticipate?) that our young will continue to romp about in their four-wheeled playpens.

These same young adults, however, have been known to rise to the occasion when they have received an affirmation of their worth and have been invited to accept responsibility as members of the human race. On the one hand, many of us are delighted to see our young embrace a full sense of respect for their sexuality, their fertility, and their capacity for developing an exclusive, lifelong relationship in marriage. On the other hand, we find no pleasure in seeing them flee from the threats of AIDS, herpes, and other sexually communicated diseases. We are part of the growing discontent with the contraceptive and abortion options touted before our children. They are the victims in this drama of premature sexual intimacy in our confused culture. My plea here is both to today's parents and to today's youth who will form tomorrow's households to live out a vision very different from that of a promiscuous culture.

### Beware a Symptom Approach

I recently participated in a symposium on teen pregnancy. Shortly after our meetings began, I concluded that I was the token voice of sexual integrity through self-discipline and commitment to exclusive, lifelong bonding. The general approach of the symposium was scientific, that is to say, the group scrutinized various data on teen pregnancies but lacked a general outlook on the problem. Repeatedly they noted—without questioning—that 50 percent of all teens between the ages of fifteen and nineteen were sexually active. Yet the actual data on teen sexual activity as provided by the National

Research Council in their 1987 book, *Risking the Future: Adolescent Sexuality, Pregnancy, and Childbearing*, breaks down like this:

| | | |
|---|---|---|
| 15-year-old | women 5.4% | men 16.6% |
| 16-year-old | women 12.6% | men 28.7% |
| 17-year-old | women 27.1% | men 47.9% |

Not until ages nineteen for women and eighteen for men do the figures reach 50 percent. I am uncomfortable speculating why people distort the data to include fifteen year olds in their blanket statement. Is seduction their actual intent or effect?

Lou Harris Associates recently completed a poll for Planned Parenthood. A major finding they reported was that students with lower-than-average grades were more likely than better performing students to be sexually active. Students performing between "F" and "C" were active at a 37 percent rate; "B-" and "B" students dropped to 25 percent; and "B+" and "A" students dropped still further to 21 percent. Note that—contrary to popular opinion—well below half of our teens are sexually active, and the rate is down to one in five for those who are doing well in school (whatever that may indicate).

We also have some returns on field research that show us what kinds of families "predict" best for launching children and young adults who are not highly susceptible to drugs, sex, and alcohol. In the spring of 1966, while I served as a consultant to an agency investigating the postponement of adolescent sexual activity, several of my students helped in the processing of data. One of them, facing marriage herself in a short time, suggested that we poll the class of forty-one students on those factors which postponed their sexual intimacy until marriage. If they were active before marriage, we asked them to indicate what factors had collapsed their restraint.

We found that 54 percent had abstained from premarital sex while the remaining 46 percent had not. We also gathered "age of conversion" data and compared this to see that many of the premaritally active students had been converted as young adults—often linking the age of conversion with the mystery and guilt of premarital relations as a likely motivation. When we listed the constraints that had prevented premarital sex, we found five spontaneous and powerful factors:

| | |
|---|---|
| Parent models | 100 percent |
| Religious teaching | 100 percent |
| Fear of pregnancy | 86 percent |
| Naivete | 43 percent |
| Nonreligious morality | 28 percent |

It was enough to send me looking for research on family dynamics and "family systems" to see how this data might combine to offer a pattern against which we could compare families and our present efforts at family life. This book is a report on what I found.

Sexual problems must be addressed at the most general level, and there is one systemic hope. It is articulated in the Judeo-Christian vision: "In the image of God they were created, male and female . . . one flesh, naked and without shame."

Lest we who are grounded in the faith communities be naive or lack courage in the face of the problems of teenage pregnancy, let us remember that the central figure in the Christian faith tradition is a man conceived out of wedlock by a young woman thought to be about sixteen years old. Unlike the popular portrayals of the church as blind or irrelevant or both, the account of that untimely pregnancy is recorded in Matthew's gospel with full attention given to the healthy reaction of Joseph. When I preach from that passage, I call the sermon, "What Shall I Do with the Baby?"

If we examine the genealogy of Jesus in that same chapter, we will see five women named or described—only five. Each of them seems to be named because she was a victim of sexually grounded tragedy: a victim of incest; a childless widow in search of another husband; a prostitute; a woman seized by a lustful king and seduced into adultery; and, last of all, Mary, a pregnant teenager whose fiance's first impulse was to end the relationship. We can only conclude that the faith communities are grounded in a tradition that is willing, even eager, to name and face the music of ultimate human dilemmas. Yet we know that we are able to do so because religion, faith, and obedience to the highest visions given to humankind are made possible by "outside help," by community support, and by radical transformation of tragedy into hope. The five women in Matthew's genealogical table call out to the troubled of all time: "Come on along! You too can be sanctified through trouble. It is a gift of grace."

## Families Make the Difference

Every generation rides on the shoulders of the previous one. The previous generation gladly furnishes the additional elevation for a better and richer perspective. Unfortunately, in this instance, we have a tendency to give today's generation a technology for sexual promiscuity when they have looked to us for support during the painful years of restraint and self-control. In one generation we have watched the emotional raping of our well-tutored youth. We have seen them grow gray and restless with trying to live out our popularized promiscuous media scenarios. They rightfully accuse us of deceiving them, of withholding the best truth of all, namely, *self-constraint is the sure foundation of lifelong fulfillment in marital and sexual maturity and satisfaction.*

This is a book about families and their best natural resource—their children. It is a book about how respect works between parent and child and between spouses—one of the single best ways of guaranteeing that a child will grow up responsible and safe. It is also a book about how to nurture maturity through early distribution of responsibility.

This book offers hope that is realistic. There are no simple formulas here, no sex education programs to guarantee that your dreams for your children will come true. Indeed the book will make it painfully clear that dreams are not enough, that it takes time and hard work to listen to children, to explain to teens, and to give them freedom and shared responsibility during the early years.

It is also a book about risk. We live in a free universe where every human being is free to make choices. These choices have consequences. So while all of us are free to choose, we

sometimes forget that we cannot choose the consequences—
they come with the choices. Since our children, like us, are
free to choose, the best parenting may not guarantee that they
will make the best choices. Our parenting, however, does
"predict" that they will make good choices, but we cannot be
guaranteed the outcome we have targeted. What we know is
that if families are driven by mutual respect and have faith-
fully distributed responsibility and accountability early
during the "launching" time, they will have the resources for
dealing with pain and tragedy as well as happiness and
celebration. The long-term prospects are excellent for these
children to affirm quickly their integrity and to have the resources for building bridges back to their parents and to the
truth. If the old proverb sometimes seems to fail us as a guaranteed formula, "Train up your children in the way they
should go and when they are adults they will not depart from
it," then the expanded version suggests, "Train up your children in the responsibility they should have and when they are
mature they will show that responsibility even if it means
coming home to the truth."

I give you the book chiefly as an invitation to break free
from self-serving and easy ways of parenting. You can discard
old ways of resisting children, and you can stop playing cat-
and-mouse games where "power" is the prize. I offer it to you
knowing that those of you, like me, who have been benevolent dictators in the citadels of your homes will welcome a
reason to change your parenting style now, at any point in
your family's life cycle. You will want to say, "Things aren't
working right, and besides, I don't like myself when I act like
this. I don't play these power games with people at work.
Let's talk about what we all need and how to proceed as
friends and responsible people." When parenting sits down
with this agenda, a new day of high respect and high distribution of responsibility will have dawned.

DONALD M. JOY, PH.D.
*Professor of Human Development*
*and Christian Education*
*Asbury Theological Seminary*
*Wilmore, Kentucky*

# 1

## *Has the World Gone Crazy or What?*

Δ

My telephone rings several times each week with anxious parents wanting to know what to do next. "Am I doing the right thing?" one father wanted to know. "I'm so angry, I'm dangerous right now," a mother reported. Another, a single parent, wailed, "I'm left with the whole load for six children, and now my high school kids seem to have blown it. Bud has turned up drunk and Aileen didn't come home at all last night." A couple turning fifty was also on the line: "Our oldest son, at twenty-five, has rescued a woman from an abusive marriage. She is now divorced, and we know they are sleeping together. Our son still lives at home, and we can tell that he is under such stress that we worry that he will snap and lose control in some tragic way. We are troubled about his role in the woman's divorce and about their sexual relationship. Sometimes we wonder whether we are going to survive ourselves." I've also heard from a frantic mother: "We've just discovered all of this pornography Bob has stashed away! I give up! Can you talk to him again?"

If those problems reflect your own fears or even a trace of the reality of your family's past or present pain, this book may

3

open windows of new hope for you. If you are a person who keeps your eye on children and youth everywhere—in a way, your only link to the future—or if you work with kids in any setting, you may be eager to unscramble the amazing tangled threads in the world of teens today. I want to give you more details on each of the five stories in this opening chapter. There are no solutions in this chapter, but the cases offer us the right issues on which to begin raising questions. If we cannot ask the best questions, we are going to run the risk of settling for inadequate answers and of hurting ourselves and the people we love by imposing flawed responses to pain and trouble.

In any event, it is hard to put today's youth out of our minds since we are all connected to them. We have created the environment in which they are at risk. Our entire linkage to the future is through them, so they will give us the future or we will have nothing at all. If God's words in the creation assigning responsibility to the original pair applies to us, then "Have dominion!" likely translates, "You're responsible!" Ultimately we and they answer to the God of history, so indifference and care-less-ness are surely not an option.

### Susie's First Date

Susie's parents are church leaders; both father and mother are graduates of a blue-chip Christian university. Her younger brother trails her by three years. When Susie hit thirteen, the parental rule rolled into place: no dating before sixteen. She complained but got nowhere. There were abundant "group dating" events at the church, and she was popular enough at school to have good social contacts.

Then in the spring of ninth grade, at age fourteen, Susie begged to be allowed to go out with Matt who had just turned sixteen, had his driver's license, and was ready to move. The miniature golf date, an hour and a half of lapsed time away from the house, seemed logical and safe. Matt's family were members of the same church, and Matt was regularly involved in the youth activities.

It was an hour and a half that still had not ended years later. Matt and Susie had sex in that hour and a half away from the house. Likely nobody will ever know just what happened, but everything changed. Susie was shattered, humiliated, and confused; she blurted everything out to her mother. Matt, confronted by his own mother after a phone call from Susie's house, admitted the episode and exploded, "Susie's nothing but a slut and a whore." In the height of anger, the words were heard at Susie's house, and they continue to ricochet through Susie's mind. Her father still has to restrain surges of violence whenever Matt's name emerges or he thinks of how Susie has changed since that evening.

Susie immediately became distant, rebellious, and deceptive. There were more boys, even without dating. The deception, however, was clumsy, and her sexual secrets repeatedly surfaced. In desperation Susie's parents began to draw up a contract with her. By the contract, Susie would agree to control her sexual adventures and her parents would agree not to go through her room looking for evidence of her behavior or try to trap her in her lies.

One night Susie's father was on the phone. "Are we doing the right thing?" He told how, after yet another deception and episode, he had simply gone silent. He avoided Susie, even around the house, vowed not to see her or to speak to her. After two days of this kind of treatment she burst into tears. "Don't do that to me. I can't stand it. At least say something!" Her father was pleased that he had found one way to get her attention.

I was listening for inferences I could make about deeper issues:

Does Susie know how much her parents love her?

Does she feel valued, respected, and honored by their love?

Have their very separate "griefs" been joined over what happened on her first date?

What are the probabilities that her sexual "acting out" can come under self-control?

What likelihood is there that it will yield to parental monitoring and control?

What resources might be available and what conditions would be required to effectively give Susie her integrity again?

What part of her rebellion is her deliberate moral choice and what part of it is simply a way to mask her devastation of self-respect?

## Joey's Best Friend

"My husband asked me to call you. Joey is nine, and yesterday his best friend next door showed him some of his father's pornographic videos and masturbated Joey. I'm so angry I'm dangerous. What will this do to Joey? Is there any way to erase what happened? I'm scared."

"How did you find out what happened?"

"I went looking for Joey and when I could hear their voices and the television going yet nobody came to the door, I walked in on them in the house. I caught them both out of their pants and the explicit sex still rolling on the video!"

"What has been Joey's response now the next day?"

"He's very quiet. He's grounded, of course, and he's angry. He isn't talking about what happened. He thinks I did the wrong thing to walk right into the neighbor's house. And I do feel a little guilty for doing that, but I was worried that something wasn't right. The boy next door seemed strange and sneaky to me somehow. Now I think I know what has messed him up."

As I listened I was wishing I knew more about Joey's relationship to his father and about the other 3,284 days of his life in his family. I was listening to Joey's mother, her panic, her anger, but I had other questions:

What resources does Joey's mother have for transforming those often destructive emotions into constructive grief, supportive conversation, and healing words for Joey?

How can a traumatic event be down-scaled and Joey's innocence returned to him through a now explicit defining of sexual feelings and sanctifying them after he has effectively been raped?

Since self-esteem damage is the first and most persistent effect on any sexual seduction, what affirmations are available to Joey just now to assure him of his value, his dignity, and his future?

*Aileen's Secret*

Aileen's father abandoned the family when Aileen was fourteen. He left in an explosive encounter that revealed he had been sustaining simultaneous sexual relationships with three other women. In a quick court action his substantial income was tapped to support the full house of elementary and high school children. Aileen is the oldest, a high school senior. She did not come home last night. Her mother had given consent for her to spend the night at a girlfriend's house only the weekend before, so at daybreak, Aileen's mother phoned there to inquire whether they had seen Aileen. The plot thickened when the other parents explained how they had given permission for their daughter to spend the night with Aileen at Aileen's house.

By noon the next day, a Saturday, Aileen was home. She was visibly shaken but not ready to talk. Confronted by the fact that her mother had data on another accomplice, the story emerged. Three guys and three girls, all seniors, had piled into a car and driven to a lake resort for an evening of alcohol and sex. Half of the teens had previous sexual experience, but Aileen and two others had their first encounters.

"I feel so abandoned," Aileen's mother said. "Her father always demanded her respect. I think she would have been afraid to try this before he left. Is there any way to get her settled down after this? What am I in for? I've got to worry now that she may be pregnant or may have picked up some disease. How should I handle my own feelings? Aileen is seventeen. What should I do to her or for her?"

I began by assuring Aileen's mother that I was ready to "weep with those who weep." Inwardly I processed questions:

What may be the connection between Aileen's father's leaving and her new sexual adventure?

What does Aileen's knowledge of her father's promiscuity do to leverage her into sexual experimentation?

What effect has the collapse of the parents' marriage had on Aileen?

How may the separation have affected her own sexual

curiosity or her awareness of potential or realized sexual pleasure?

Could Aileen's sudden change of character and the lost night at the lake cottage have been at some level an expression of rage directed toward her father or even toward her mother for not fixing the marriage long ago?

The past, however, cannot be repaired. Here is Aileen. Now. In this present world. She needs help. Her sense of self is shattered at least twice: the loss of her father and a night of sexual curiosity with five people who invaded her citadel of privacy with the help of a tantalizing conspiracy and the deadening of her remaining inhibitions by the masking power of alcohol.

### Ed and Mary's Heartbreak

When Randy graduated from high school, he was honored to be awarded a Julliard scholarship. This took him immediately from the family nest into the very narrow professional track of musical performance. He moonlighted easily in music performance. His parents gladly supported this obvious trajectory into a life vocation of his first love: music. Randy was home, of course, for holidays and at least briefly each summer, so the family vacations and high events continued to be important to Randy and his younger sister.

Randy did not complete the music degree because a job opened near home that was hooked into music publishing and recording. It did not pay well, but he loved the environment and the people. That is where he found Donna, withering on the vine of an abusive marriage. Randy's stable character and his gentleness were a magnet to Donna, and he found himself aiding her to get out of her marriage. The pity evoked a quick seduction, and Randy and Donna were involved sexually.

Ed and Mary were beside themselves. Randy was caught needing to be with Donna and yet living at home. He was caught between needing to be a man of truth and wanting privacy in pursuing marriage with a woman he personally delivered from an abusive marriage. "We're torn between thinking we should put him out of the house and tell him to come home only when he becomes an honest man, and feeling so committed to him that we fear for his sanity and know we cannot throw him out." I walked around the scenario with Ed and Mary:

What signs are there that Randy is committed to truth and integrity?

What alternatives do you think Randy sees open to him in the present mix of sexual, marital, financial, and emotional realities?

When a child is twenty-five, what role can parents play in their children's decisions? How does Randy regard your values and your concerns?

If he seems deceptive, is the apparent lying motivated by the moral stress Randy is carrying or by the need for privacy as he constructs a bond with a troubled woman?

### Bob's Inner Vacuum

Five years ago I found myself responding to an anxious mother who wanted me to talk with her son who was failing his seventh-grade subjects. My wife, Robbie, and I enjoy contact with several faith communities in central Kentucky, and this family came through one of those many settings where I lead seminars about the family.

Nell brought Bob to see me on three occasions. I explained to her that I would meet with him on two conditions: (1) Bob would choose to talk to me, instead of being brought against his will, and (2) I would not discuss with his mother anything Bob said to me; I would protect his information and would only provide for her a general evaluation of Bob's situation and progress.

The strategy worked quite well. Bob's next grading period saw him pull the semester out of a slump. Down the five years he has succeeded well. In addition, armed with my phone number, Bob initiated an average of one extended phone consultation or report each month across the years. Then, when he turned sixteen, he showed up at our house both to show off a car and to report in and pose his current questions. He was a frequent guest in our home. Occasionally he showed up when I was out of town for a few days and would show a mild irritation that I was not there when he needed to talk.

The strategy, however, was flawed from the beginning on a higher level. I discovered some seriously stressed family relationships in Bob's story. So not long ago, during Bob's senior year of high school, his mother phoned again in a panic to report yet another instance of Bob's recent unacceptable behavior. I asked to see the entire family of five.

I went to their home for the session. Bob's picture of his relationship to each parent and to each sibling had prepared me to ask some questions, all centered on their perception of Bob's recent disruptive behavior. My questions evoked clear and coherent responses from all four witnesses, but I noticed that Bob's mother was nervous and tense, except when she spoke. Often she visibly restrained herself from interrupting to take over the responses of the other family members. It was clear that the major conflict in the family was between the parents, and the three children were making very different responses to the dynamics in that marriage.

Bob made another unannounced visit to our home. This time he was almost in shock that a recent week away from his family found him vulnerable to very destructive substances and behaviors. "I had this feeling that my parents were 200 miles away, and I could do anything I wanted to do. But I didn't really want to be doing any of them! It's like I just felt hollow in here," he said, pointing to his chest, "and I had no control. Do you think I can get this fixed?" I take Jesus seriously in John 20 and, with a free confession like Bob's, gladly announced his sins "forgiven," but I told him that the hollowness may come from something else.

In the next breath he told me that he felt guilty about a major flare-up at home six months prior. His parents had demanded that he turn over his paycheck from his part-time job. They also demanded that he empty his billfold, asking, "Is this all the money you have?" Bob lied. He had hidden away nearly $200 in his room trying to save $500 just as a nest egg. Now he was in trouble because he did not dare tap into the money; they would demand to know how he had any spending money.

How do you say to a seventeen-year-old that his need to take responsibility for his own life is important when his parents' idea of giving him responsibility is to punish him by adding penalty family chores: washing, ironing, and doing dishes? The responsibility he needs may include carrying a full share of the family's chores, but it has to include being responsible for the management of a reasonable amount of money.

It was not surprising that Bob felt hollow in the middle. That is where his self-responsibility should have been housed, and he was bankrupt at seventeen and had no way of resisting seductions of virtually any kind.

That's when he dropped the bomb: "My sister is using laxatives every day to lose weight." I had seen it coming, I guess. This family system was turning out more and more symptoms of its troubled nature. Bob had been into drugs, alcohol, marijuana, pornography, and tobacco. His sister had stepped into anorexia nervosa. This family system, like so many of our families, was putting its most treasured resources "at risk" to major destructive patterns that are preying on young people today.

### A Collision of Flawed Moralities

It is sometimes said that we stand between the old morality and the new morality. The so-called new morality is said to have set the stage for sexual liberation.

Play off the old and the new for a moment to see them in contrast. If these older and newer ways of looking at sexual activity do, in fact, arm us with two different sets of rules, then we can understand the problems in the four families I described to open this chapter. Here they are in contrast.

### New Morality

1. If it feels good, do it. If you want to be sexual with anyone, it is your right.
2. If there is no pregnancy and no disease, there is no moral issue.

### Old Morality

1. If it feels good, it is evil. All sexual desire is evil, even within marriage, and should be curbed except for reproduction.

2. Fornication and adultery irrevocably bring an end to life on this planet as you have known it.

It is hard to imagine two positions that are more explosive when stated in contrast to each other. It is equally difficult to try to invent any position that is more potentially destructive of the human spirit than either the so-called new morality or the old morality as expressed here. Surely there is a more humane and God-designed view of sexual integrity and sexual responsibility. We would expect to find it grounded in the oldest and best of our faith perspectives. We should expect to find that what works best with humans is consistent with the deepest understandings about how God creates us and calls to us in creation, redemption, and holy Scripture.

## Grounding for an Ultimate Moral Base

What emerges when we go in search of a truly humane and God-given moral foundation is remarkably different both in tone and in direction:

### Ultimate Morality

1. Human sexuality is very good. It is a free gift for cementing an exclusive, lifelong monogamous family.
2. Sexual experience is sustained with pleasure, grounded in bonding and communication, and accompanied by health-giving brain chemicals guaranteeing the ideal matrix for high quality of life and for creating new life.
3. Genital contact in an exclusive marital setting laminates sexual pleasure to the person, full responsibility for that person from that day forward, eagerness to establish long-range privacy and independence and to pay the "rent" to sustain that new one-flesh unit of the human race. Genital contact without marriage, however, tends to bond the sexual pleasure to secretive, illegal, irresponsible conspiracy so that later marriage is easily flawed by promiscuity that goes in search of the original "buzz" of the illegal, secret rendezvous.

*In Search of Integrity*

I have offered these five embryonic cases in an opening chapter as an invitation to you. By them, I want you to feel drawn to bring the most troublesome problem you face or the most worrisome prospect that might come to your family. When our kids are stepping into adulthood we often act out of fear or out of simple reflex, and much of the time we realize too late that we have made a small problem bigger. Occasionally we respond in ways that seem to change things for the better.

As the book unfolds you will see new possibilities for turning normal family fears into some quiet hope—based on both facts about the kids and about handling our fears. The heart of the matter will open up as we X-ray your family structure and look at some predictors that tend to show up in building a strong and healthy family.

# 2

# *The First Curriculum*

△

Mark was the fourthborn and third son. In many ways he was lucky. His only sister was fourteen—just blossoming into womanhood and ready to be a "second mother" and give him extra attention. His oldest brother was sixteen. There were, however, complications.

Mark's mother did not have sufficient breast milk to feed him, and he was allergic to synthetic formulas and cow's milk. The family doctor, however, knew of a neighboring family with a newborn. So Mark went every day to nurse at the breast of a woman five miles away. I was seven then and was often in Mark's home because his next oldest brother was my best friend.

As Mark came into toddlerhood, it was clear that we had on our hands a high energy fellow who was clever and quick. I don't know what the actual arrangement was, but I heard that Mark's father was "going to raise this one." Perhaps his mother was so exasperated with Mark that she shifted responsibility to the father, but the chemistry between Mark and his father was not good. I recall Mark's near-violent response when his father would put him off with a simple and crisp, "'Cause!" as a put-down to avoid giving explanations to

Mark's many questions. In his frustration at what amounted to no answer to his boyish curiosity, Mark would shriek, "'Cause is a crows' reason! I want to know why!"

What we watched unfold, however, was a pattern of irregular behavior. The three older children were pleasant, peaceable, and comfortable in standard social behavior. When he was later at college, Mark was quickly in serious legal trouble for interfering with railroad signals. His cleverness and his irregular value system left all of us guessing at what the next turn might be. Late in his twenties, he abandoned his wife and family and parents. After several years he contacted his mother and father. The lifelong painful pattern of isolation and alienation, however, has come at a high price for all of us who know Mark.

Contrast Mark's story with that of Jim. Jim, too, almost starved to death at his mother's breast. The pediatrician quickly shifted him to bottle-feeding to supplement the short supply of mother's milk. Childhood and adolescence were smooth. Parents were best friends, confidants, and front-row cheerleaders at all extracurricular activities. Off to college, in the blush of new freedom, Jim did some experimentation beyond the family's value system. Then, during a spring break came this disclosure: "Some of the guys said their dads would kill them if they knew what they were doing. But I told them mine wouldn't kill me. 'If my dad knew what I was doing he wouldn't kill me, but it would probably kill him.'"

All of us who live in "family" wonder what we can do to make a difference with our children. Living, as we do, in a culture full of booby traps that threaten to explode the values and beliefs many of us hold dear, we have come to ask whether these may be days in which it might be better to remain childless. Yet at some level most of us know that those instincts are cowardly, that the world needs our kind of families and needs our children to make a difference. We are eager to do our best. Each of us holds secretly to the dream we heard articulated in the old marriage litany, and we want to establish and sustain a home that is, indeed, "a haven of blessing, and a place of peace."

In this chapter I want to deal with the "first curriculum." In choosing that language, I mean to emphasize that three basic gifts make up the first and most powerful experiences of education and formation. I do not mean to suggest that parents are following a textbook in their parenting. I am speaking of an even more powerful curriculum: the unwritten one that creates the basic environment for the child. It punctuates the air with sounds of instruction, praise, and accountability. As you can see, my thesis is that each of us has been given a set of basic life experiences that amounts to a basic "curriculum" for our formation and maturing. When we prepare a résumé or a vita on ourselves, a competent secretary will likely type it up as "John Jones, Curriculum Vitae." Here, again, "curriculum" refers to the life experiences of John Jones.

We know that what the curriculum does depends in part on the learner. So the variation in response is not entirely predictable. That basic curriculum consists of three things: parents, intimacy, and personal sexuality.

## The Gift of Parents

When an infant arrives on this planet, its life is a direct gift from two parents: one adult male and one adult female. At the simplest level possible, we could conclude that both of these parents are important if the infant's world is to be complete and whole.

These two adults will provide an enormous life experience curriculum to the child. Consider the content of those "courses of study" under the tutorial care of parents:

1. How valuable I am.
2. What a man is.
3. What a woman is.
4. How a man and a woman relate to each other.
5. How needs are met.
6. How safe the world is.
7. How to keep responsibilities.
8. How to wait for things I really want.
9. Who you can trust.
10. How competent I am.

Don't you wish you could write the curriculum for a lot of troubled people you know as adults? Can you see how a good foundation curriculum in the years from birth to fifteen might "risk proof" your child? Look now at a list of ways the curriculum is administered:

1. By voice.
2. By touch.
3. By gesture and body language.
4. By spontaneous living out of adult roles and responsibilities.
5. By faithfulness in providing basic care and emotional support for the child.
6. By giving feedback to the child at the level of obedience, of performance, and of simply being your child.
7. By giving exposure to and interpretation of the outside, not-always-trustworthy world.

Try to take the perspective of a two-year-old child. Put yourself on the floor to lower your sense of power and influence. Imagine watching the transactions going on between your parents. You have had the almost undivided attention of your mother for the last hour. The door has just opened and this "other" person, your father, has come into the room. You take a deep breath and may even be startled with his abrupt entrance into your world. Especially if you are a boy, you may be magnetically drawn to him, quickly scooting to your feet and taking off to tackle him at the knees, demanding his attention. If he is a reminder of gentle but very different "father care," you will be ready to appeal for his attention as a supplement to the care you have had from your mother. Yet it is not to happen now. Your mother and father are in each other's arms. He is whispering in her ear. She squeals lightly and goes for the phone. You hear her dialing, then talking to "Grandma." "Of course, tonight! It's our anniversary!"

Suddenly you sense that you are going to be abandoned. It has happened before. Grandma is coming again. She will read to you, and it will be bedtime soon. What will happen to mother and father? Why is it that sometimes when father comes home he takes mother away?

*What a mother does.* The connection between a mother and a child tends to be so well established both by physical origin and by extended time that in infancy the child cannot imagine itself separate from the mother. Indeed "egocentrism" as defined by the famed researcher Jean Piaget did not refer to a self-centered child, but rather to a child whose tunnel vision imagined that the only world that exists is the child's perceived world. In this child's world it is the child who does not exist, since the child has no awareness of self. Children's drawings of their families, up into ages six or seven, often are remarkable in one common feature: they omit themselves from the drawings of their families. They can name family members, but they tend to forget to include themselves.

Watch a mother hold a baby—cradling it in her left arm. She will find this position instinctual, often working and holding the baby with ease. As the baby grows into a toddler, she tends to scoop the child up in one or another of these intimate "encompassing" positions. The curriculum message is easily "security." To be safe is to be in mother's arms. In the Judeo-Christian tradition God's care for the people of God is often compared to that of a mother for her children, whether Israel or the church. Both are also viewed as wife and bride of the deity, and both form the encompassing, birthing, nurturing mother care at the community level.

*What a father does.* The connection between the father and the child lacks the nine months of literal physical connection. Mothers clock more hours with children than do fathers. This time investment difference produces an amazing effect. On the one hand, in its egocentrism, the young child very early cannot distinguish between the mother and the self but does distinguish between the father and the mother-self unit. On the other hand, Daddy is the outsider, the wholly other who comes and goes, who intrudes into the mother-child attachment. Sometimes the father grasps the infant and takes it away from the mother, but sometimes the father takes the mother away from the infant. In either case, the images of power and control tend to create a concept of "male as fearful, sometimes playful, but always good and safe, wholly other."[1]

Watch a father play with his child. The urge to cradle the child against the abdomen tends to fade and the father moves the infant perpendicular to his own frame, cupping its head in his hands, which seem just made for the size of that small cranium. By the clock, fathers spend larger proportions of time "en face" (face to face) with their children than do mothers who tend to cradle them more of the time.[2] With the toddler, whom the mother still tends to hold affectionately and to balance now on the hip, the father goes to the floor and gives himself to the child in rollicking play. Wild monsters and wrestling matches in which the child can subdue the father in triumph, seem built into a father's repertoire of parenting gifts. From perhaps six months to late toddlerhood, the child will experience the adventures of flight as the father hoists the little one. First it is a test of perpendicularity and balance, then the playful toss introduces the child to the full release of flight. These father games stress the child by combining the adventure of fear and the certainty of father's strong hands. A major test of every person's faith comes with the question of whether God exists, and if so, whether he is whimsical or good. Children whose fathers have experienced this repertory of father play have passed their first course in "a theology of the wholly Other," and they tend to find faith in the God who is both fearsome and good. It is a relatively easy hurdle in the journey of faith.

### The Gift of Intimacy

In our search for curriculum, life experiences that teach, it is clear that the parent-child transactions are rich with content. Nothing is more urgent than what the child infers from intimate contact with both parents.

*The skin.* Contact involving actual skin connection is more powerful communication than that involving words with the young child. I am basically put off by the debate about whether to smack a child with the hand or with a "rod," but part of the argument rests on a powerful reality: the parent's hand is the primary symbol of affection through touch.

Stroking the child's skin while it is being fed, bathed, or changed evokes the most positive sensations for the child as well as for the adult. Ask yourself what the message of touch is.

Early in my graduate teaching experience Robbie and I hosted a couples' support group in our home after church on Wednesday nights. One morning I saw one of the men in animated conversation near the campus post office. I was in a hurry, but wanted to signal him that I had seen him without interrupting his conversation with his two friends. As I passed, it was easy to reach out and lay my right hand on his arm just above the wrist. The whole touch could not have lasted more than a second. Yet the next Wednesday, Bill brought it up with the group. "I don't know what you intended to be saying to me when you touched me in the hallway last week." I asked whatever he was talking about. He recited the details. "That is something I would do, I'm sure, but I don't remember the event at all."

"Well," he went on, "all over me I suddenly felt important. I felt that you really liked me, and I have rarely felt better about myself than I did for several minutes after you passed by."

In any search for self-esteem it will be important to weigh the importance of touch. Look at the ways parents make galvanic contact with the child's skin.

1. Holding
2. Stroking
3. Kissing
4. Bathing
5. Diapering

*The mouth.* Very early the child learns to return mouth-to-mouth contact with an open mouth, often imitating its nursing/feeding action by offering a slobbery kiss. The mother's breast provides a ring of tactile sensation to the nursing baby. Even with bottle-fed babies, mothers seem instinctively to know that they need to be held, cuddled, stroked, and talked to while feeding. The breast-mouth contact, however, must surely provide an additional tranquilizing affirmation. That skin connection telegraphs acceptance, dependency, even pleasure. It laminates all of those positive sensations to the satisfaction of the child's primary cry of hunger. For the abundantly lactating mother there is relief, too, at the release of the milk when its ripening has made her uncomfortable.

*The genitals.* The cleansing routine, whether with cleaning oil or soapy water, offers an opportunity for the excitement of total touch, with all the sensations that make for well-being. Diapering, with the necessary cleansing of the rectal and genital area, frequently evokes kicking and squealing for sheer delight—the delight of freedom, for one, but the delight may also be related to the affirmation of nonerotic sexuality. In God's creation, all mammals provide early genital affirmation. In some lower animals it is believed that the genital contact is what provokes brain chemicals essential to life. The least we can do is to acknowledge that the long dependency of the child and the parenting instincts in humans that favor stroking, kissing, and encompassing the child provide a most powerful curriculum. The curriculum content is acceptance, affirmation, and celebration of being.

## The Gift of Sexuality

The child's sexual endowment may provide the most persistent of all curricula. This unfolding saga of highly personal learning experiences begins, perhaps, with an awareness of sexual identity. It expands to learning the sex role, then to the amazing changes of pubescence, and finally to the affirmation of adult sexual responsibility both for intimacy and for procreation. Yet the curriculum is not finished. It extends to the messages of sexual waning at mid-life, eventually to the end of fertility for women and to a higher risk for problems in sexual performance for men. Both are reminders of the waning of time in the life sequence.

*Sexual identity.* Who knows when or how the young child, barely a toddler, picks up the idea of its own sexual identity? Our first glimpses of the evidence evoke a smile. The child expresses clear preferences for "same sex" parent time or attention. At eighteen months, Justin had learned to lift the window curtain early in the morning, inspect the driveway, and deduce whether his father was still in the house. If both vehicles were there, he would remain silent and pretend to be asleep waiting for Mike to pick him up for diapering and for breakfast. If Dorian, his mother, would come for him, he would resist, whimper "Daddy," and "awaken" happily when Mike would come for him. When, at three, he enrolled in the Montessori school, he still had a deal going with his father by which they would sometimes conspire to miss a day of school in order to be "partners." This sense of maleness and of strong preference to be in the company of the father is clearly an identity that develops before genital awareness, before instruction, and before social pressures. We seem to stand in awe of the mystery of sexual identity. The child's sexual identity is easily the child's farthest reaching lever on the feelings of worth, acceptability, and celebration.

*Sex role.* Here we see the child's experience surface as it intentionally imitates the "sex appropriate" gestures, carriage, dress, and speech of older, often adult, same sex people. Parents are the earliest models for this curriculum. Their values, preferences, and patterns show up as if by carbon copy in the child. Sometimes there is a clear shouldering of the load of adult sex role as you listen in on children:

"I hate girls, but I know I've got to get married sometime, because if I don't, it's the end of the Jones name."

"How do you make gravy? I know I'm going to have to learn how to make gravy some day."

Turn the kids loose in the attic with a box of clothing you are ready to turn into scrap. Be sure there are shoes and hats as well as more basic apparel. Or watch the play area at a day-care center where options exist to take up imitative adult tools or toys. Sex role preferences are distinctly shaped by the culture, but the curriculum is innate; children are eager to pick up skills and to experiment with feelings rooted in "trying it."

*Pubescence.* With the onset of pubescence the child turns into a distinct sexual person: a woman or a man. Before that two-year period of bodily change, boys and girls resemble each other in body mass and configuration. Only the genitals tell the genetic difference. As musculature is enhanced in boys and fatty tissue reformats the girl's body, the curriculum screams the message of maturing sexuality. The boy's voice cracks and lowers, pubic hair sprouts along with hair in the armpits. The girl's breasts bud and pubic hair appears. The end of pubescence arrives with the first menstrual cycle for the girl and with first ejaculation for the boy.

What does the curriculum say now? It says basically: You are no longer a child. You are capable of reproduction. Your sexuality now not only guarantees your sexual identity, it predicts for you a posterity. Fertility is an enormous gift. "I could become a mother!" "I could make a baby!" are both discoveries of power and the threshold of responsibility. With the ripening of the sexual system also comes an almost parallel maturing of the brain. Reflective, evaluative questioning now raises questions about meaning, responsibility, and readiness for being an adult. The emerging adolescent is now ready to entertain life's largest questions:

1. Faith/Belief
2. Vocation
3. Sexual Responsibility
4. Marriage and Family.

When the child has been positively affirmed by the parent curriculum and when the intimacy curriculum has further confirmed the child's worth and capability, it predicts for early faith commitment, vocational vision, and sense of sexual responsibility—and its relationship to plans for marriage and family.

When I opened this subject recently with a group of ministers, one woman volunteered afterward, "I always imagined that my experience was unique. But the week I felt my call to ministry was also the week of my first period. Now, I suspect you are right. It was connected to my sense of the arrival of womanhood."

Men frequently tell the same sort of story. G. Gayle Stephens speaking at a Greenville College chapel several years ago, described how he and his roommate, Moses Flowers, struggled with the idea of "entire sanctification." The two of them made many spiritual adventures during those college years in search of inward holiness. He reported that he now suspected that the motor driving his spiritual quest during those college years was his sexual energy. The quest for entire sanctification was largely motivated by that unresolved moral and spiritual battle of sexual imagination and desire. He smiled at the naiveté of that probability. When we consider other ways of dealing with emerging adult sexual energy, however, there is perhaps no other way so likely to lead to responsible choices about fertility, the pursuit of intimacy, and marriage.

If, on the other hand, the child is unsure of its value, or if the intimacy curriculum has been inconsistent or has been punctuated by abusive punishment, then the adolescent's engagement of life's larger questions is frequently characterized by rejection, confusion, avoidance, and irresponsibility.

*Adult sexuality.* Whether healthy or deformed, the agenda of establishing significant and exclusive attachment with a sexual partner becomes critical at the turn from the second to the third decade of life. So demanding is the sexual intimacy agenda that both men and women know it expresses the core personality. "Till death do us part" is the instinctive commitment that healthy sexual contact affirms.

Adult sexual intimacy carries with it also the clear sense of responsibility for human fertility and for bearing the responsibility for pregnancy and nurturance of one's own child. Healthy young adults embrace all this, given their magnetic pull toward the prospect of their unborn young. Last summer, with six young backpackers, we each predicted where we would be in ten years, what our faith and family commitments would be, and what our vocations would be. The boys ranged in age from twelve to sixteen. Their projections seemed to be squarely grounded in their family and intimacy curriculums from earliest childhood. The son of a remarried divorcee who had just returned from two months with his natural father, but rejoiced that his mother had married "a Christian step-father who really cares about me," expressed the belief that he would still be single at twenty-five. "I don't want to make a mistake by marrying somebody I can't really love, and besides I want to make a lot of money before I get married." On the other hand, a twelve-year-old predicted that he would be married at twenty-two and "probably have at least one child, because my parents married early like that, and I want to be able to enjoy my children while I am still young. I'll still be in a Ph.D. program in herpetology, but that's no big deal."

Adults who are fully responsible are careful to laminate their sexual pleasure to full responsibility not only for fertility but for the life and fortunes of marriage and running a household. Sexual pleasure without responsibility, quite abundant in our culture, separates maximum pleasure from maximum responsibility. This separation is a sort of schizophrenia by which any future effort to marry is flawed by the tendency for the bond to break when the going gets tough. On the other hand, when sexual pleasure is fully integrated with legal and economic responsibility for the relationship, the marriage is virtually indestructible and is literally "till death do us part."

*Mid-life and declining sexual energy.* In the typical life sequence the woman's fertility begins to sputter by irregular ovulation within a few years of the transition at the end of the fourth decade of life. A male's hormonal level typically begins to decline in the twenties but does not show up in significantly lower sexual performance or genital configuration until well past the woman's typical menopause. Should surgery alter either the breasts of the woman or the reproductive system of the man, they are likely to become aware that the "core of personality" is under siege, that they are somehow and mysteriously diminished, that they are less than they were meant to be.

Erik Erikson was right. The issue now is "ego integrity." The sex system is again the curriculum, and its content now revolves around "what truly constitutes personhood?" If being a baby maker is the primary source of feelings of worth for a woman, then menopause can pose an enormous threat to any sense of self-worth. If being a sexual giant or a playboy has focused on genital performance, a man will feel that life on this planet is ending for him. If his ego strength remains chiefly attached to sexual prowess, we are likely to see some desperate mid-life bids for recapturing his adolescent potency. The "affair," the mid-life "binge," and other forms of craziness are signals that the insecure and aging adult has not achieved integrity.

In this chapter, I have wanted you to consider that we have been given a first curriculum that is primarily without words, books, or supplementary media resources. The first curriculum for each of us comes to us in the care and support we are given by our parents. The early experiences of affirmation or rejection and abuse that arise out of intimate encounters are also a factor. Finally, the gift of our individual sexuality and how it is played out across the life span is involved.

There is no foolproof way of guaranteeing that the most positive construction of the first curriculum will produce healthy and responsible children. There is every evidence that carelessness in this first curriculum correlates very strongly with lifelong irresponsibility. So as we embark on this journey of looking at ways of launching children in an age of irresponsibility and promiscuity, it has been necessary to start here. There are, however, miles to go before we are through surveying the resources available to us if we would be responsible parents today.

## QUESTIONS PEOPLE ASK

**Q:** *You confuse me a little by calling parents the first curriculum. I think parents are supposed to teach God's first curriculum: how to be a good person, how to come to know God, and how to live. Mostly I think of parents as teachers, not as curriculum.*

**A:** There is an old German proverb, "Don't do as I do, do as I say." So I am going to hold firm in suggesting that God has created us in such a way that we teach much more by "being" than by "talking." I am using first curriculum to suggest that we need to consider the magnificent way God has formed the family so that we are always teaching simply by being a man or by being a woman. It is that simple.

Words, of course, are important as vehicles of interpretation, but we depend on words for only about 5 percent of all communication. The other 95 percent of meaning comes from body language, gestures, tone, inflection, and the whole-person messages that emerge as we speak. You have had the experience of actually saying something you never intended to say, yet your friends understood you because 95 percent of your communication was overpowering the wrong word. They may have corrected you, but not abruptly, because they understood *you* perfectly well. The first curriculum is like that. It is what we telegraph with 95 percent of our energy that does the most lasting and most powerful teaching.

*Q: Frankly, I am a little tired of everything being reduced to sex. We get enough of that from television and the movies. Even the news is sickening with its preoccupation with sex and sexual diseases. Now you say it is the first curriculum. I find that hard to accept.*

A: I resonate with your objections, completely. I object, however, even more to the exploitation of God's grandest gift—our sexuality. You and I would have been more comfortable if we could have left sex in the bedroom and especially in the bridal chamber where it survived for centuries almost without a vocabulary for describing it. I'm afraid that the exploitation of the gift of intimacy has made it necessary for us to develop a vocabulary for describing the most enhancing aspect of our human existence. If we don't, then suicides and human misery will mount higher and higher as people feel deceived by the media that seduced them, dehumanized them, and exploited them.

Read about the ultimate seduction of the innocent in the "great harlot" passage of your Bible: Revelation 17 and 18. Then read about the "bride dressed in white." The good news is so overpowering that evil simply disintegrates and crumbles away in the presence of the good, the true, and the holy. So this is another book about God's creation of what is good, true, and holy. I think we can take a deep breath and survive even if we have to use sexual images such as bride and groom in contrast to ugly words like harlot and seduction.

# 3

## *All Dressed Up and No Place to Go!*

△

I have committed a few acts of violence in my life. I have been able to make restitution for some. For others, I will do a lifetime of penance. There is, however, a singular episode that sometimes comes back to haunt me.

Rockwall, Texas was a sleepy little county seat town in the early 1950s. Like many such places, there wasn't much to do, but what you heard tended to make up for it. We had been serving a small congregation there for only a few weeks when the gossip line raised the question of whether I was getting my fair share of the marriage industry for which the community had a negative reputation.

The question at least put into perspective the fact that on a recent Saturday, two couples, total strangers to me, had appeared at the parsonage door requesting that I marry them. Neither training nor experience had prepared me for such a request, so I graciously invited them in, interrogated them as to their commitment to God, examined their credentials, and married them.

After a few months it became clear that some of the clergy in town had a "pipeline" that ran all the way from the courthouse to their offices. One minister boasted that he made more from marriage fees in a year than from his salary. The motor in this marriage mill had two cylinders: a medical clinic open twenty-four hours a day and a night watchman who was authorized to issue marriage licenses after hours and all night. I quickly devised a better screening system to regulate the trickle of couples who missed the conveyer belt that ran from the clinic and court house to the "marrying ministers."

One Saturday (a good day to be out of town) our family was making its exit only to almost literally bump into a young couple. They were timid souls, looking at their feet much too much, I'm afraid. The young man spoke.

"We want to get married."

"Do you have a license?"

"No, sir. When we got the medical exams paid for we were out of money. Could you help us with the two dollars to get the license, and then would you marry us?"

And here I committed my atrocity: "If you don't have money for a license, then you surely aren't ready to get married, are you?" They turned and walked up the street as we drove away.

So there I was, in cold blood. I asked no questions about age, about motivation, about their support network of important people, about money or job back home. On the edge of sleep some nights, I still see them turning to walk away. I never asked their names. I wonder where they are and whether anyone at all cared about them as persons or respected whatever integrity was driving them to a Saturday marriage in Rockwall, Texas.

When it comes time to talk about marriage, our culture is almost reflexively materialistic. We accuse primitive and third world cultures of being preoccupied with dowry, money, and cows as "bride price," but we have our own telltale symptoms of familial greed.

Yet, in a word, the people involved are the most precious and nonreplaceable components in the wedding negotiation. Time, money, and convenience evaporate as values when we consider that if we miss our timing with our young, we may damage, even destroy, the best resources we will ever have.

Their innocence, their integrity, and their single-minded devotion peak with young love. In this chapter we want to sweep open the door to let them through, "all dressed up with no place to go."

## Mixed Signals to the Young

"What do you think you are, a little kid?"

"Absolutely not! You're no adult! What makes you think you have a right even to ask such a thing?"

Both of these responses tend to be hurled at exactly the same person. We expect a twelve-year-old to behave like the adult that seems to have appeared in that child's body. We are, however, slow to grant that a twelve-year-old might want to schedule some of the day's activity independent of the family.

None of us is going to live long enough to get a perspective on human development or what is best for the human race. It is easy to believe that the way it is is the way it is supposed to be. What is even more surprising is that most of the time we cannot imagine that defining adulthood might ever have been different from the way we do it now in our culture. Take the following test to see if we seem to be pretty confused right now in Western European and North American culture. Indeed, it is easier to become an adult in New Guinea today than in these fine technological cultures we enjoy.

The test is on the facing page. In it you will name the age boundary across which the child steps to enter adult status.

What do you think? When is a child an adult? The answer, of course, depends on what day of the week it is, and what the kid wants. What could be more convenient to the power brokers—parents, merchants, and society at large? How could we confuse children more? Until modern times, namely the last one hundred years, children knew for sure the day, or the week, or the year when they entered adult status. I want to trace the development of our modern confusion, but let me tell you that what we have created for ourselves is a monster for which we have the devil to pay. Erik Erikson has called

# Welcome to the Adult World!

*Fees Paid*

    1. Age at which a child must order from the adult menu in your favorite restaurant? _____

    2. Age at which a child must be counted at an adult rate if checking into a motel with the family or must pay adult fare on an air line? _____

    3. Age at which gate admissions shift from child to adult rate for concerts, athletic events, or tractor pulls? _____

*Medical Status*

    4. Age at which dosage on aspirin changes to "adult"? _____

    5. Age at which all over-the-counter drugs break off "child dosage" and begin "adult dosage"? _____

*Legal Status*

    6. Age at which a person may be licensed to operate a motor vehicle in your state? _____

    7. Age at which a person may legally purchase liquor? _____

    8. Age at which a person may vote in state and national elections? _____

    9. Age at which a person may be drafted by selective service? _____

    10. Age at which a person may be convicted of a felony? _____

    11. Age at which a person may work without a "work permit"? _____

*Spiritual Competency*

    12. Age at which a person may be converted? _____

    13. Age at which Jewish ceremonies of passage are conducted? _____

    14. Age at which children are "confirmed" or given believer's baptism? _____

List here the "range" of ages from above: _____

List here the "average" age from above: _____

it "the psychosocial moratorium" by which we turn our backs on our young and try not to notice their childish mismanagement of social and moral responsibility. We protect them from legal or media consequences because of their age, but also hold them beyond dignity and responsibility everywhere. So they invent their own categories of dignity, their fads, their heroes, and their lifestyles. We call the blackout years "adolescence." We have invented it.[1]

### The Postponement of Responsibility

Before we get to defining and "inventing" adolescence, we need to get a perspective on human history. We looked at the irrational way we define "child" and "adult" in the Western world today. What does not come to mind easily is this shocking fact: *Humans have not always reared and launched their young as we now rear and launch them.*

We know the truth of such a statement at some level, but we have no place in which to stand to see farther back than the knowledge of our own childhoods which were gleaned from the folklore our parents told us of their own and their parents' stories. Mostly we are regaled by the shopworn complaints of, "When I was your age, I had to walk five miles to school through a blizzard." Unless we check the family record in the Bible on the coffee table, we rarely notice a change in the age at which they dropped out of school and went to work—or the age at which they married. If we had the data on these for all of our ancestors, we would begin to see that each of us contains a sort of genetic record of the change in ways of living and launching children.

Many of us have looked into our family genealogies enough to find that as our early American ancestors traveled West by wagon train they dropped off mid-teen adolescents to work or marry along the way. Our family tree has branches in Pennsylvania, Ohio, Missouri, and Kansas; only the youngest child made it to California with the parents.

Ronald L. Koteskey has given us his *Understanding Adolescence,*[2] in which he has traced the history of teenage responsibility. What is almost unimaginable is that as recently as a hundred years ago, children were regarded as adults almost instantly, overnight. There was no adolescence in such a time, just as there is no adolescence now in many cultures; children became adults by a social event that bestowed instant responsibility on them.

I wrote a chapter for Roy B. Zuck and Warren S. Benson in their *Youth Education in the Church.* I called it "Adolescents in Socio-Psychological Perspective." In it my opening line read: "Jesus was once a teen-ager, but he was never an adolescent." The editors whacked that line, so the sentence was published in 1968, watered down: "It may be that adolescence is produced by modern societies and technology."[3]

What we may have in Jesus' visit to the Temple in Jerusalem at age twelve[4] (Luke 2:41–52) is his parents' being caught in the middle about who was responsible for the boy's whereabouts. It was common in cross-country caravan travel of that time for the women to leave before the men, who would leave just in time to overtake the women before nightfall and the setting up of overnight accommodations. Mary could easily have said, "Well, Jesus is old enough to be with the men." Likewise, Joseph could have assumed that Jesus had gone on, as children traditionally did, with the women's caravan. Yet, at age twelve, he was likely thought to be competent to take responsibility for his transportation, even to choosing which of the caravans to join. Try to trade places with Mary and Joseph.

What would you think and do if your child had been missing for three days and nights before you finally found him?

What would you do with him? To him?

Today we would be inclined to report Mary and Joseph to Social Services or to the police for child abuse or negligence. We likely have a swatch of real life that tells us that the parents of Jesus' day knew certain things that we have lost sight of in our culture. Trace some of the shocking elements that collide with our popular ideas about preadolescent twelve-year-olds:

1. Mary and Joseph assumed that a twelve-year-old could make judgments about life, health, and safety and that he would be responsible for knowing the caravan schedule and making it to the departure gate on time.

2. When you go looking for "missing" twelve-year-olds you expect to find them in intergenerational environments characterized by safety because everyone respects, takes seriously, and regards as adults all children in the age twelve transitional year.
3. This twelve-year-old was comfortable with adults, knowing how to ask good questions and how to listen to the wisdom of older folk.
4. Everyone who heard this twelve-year-old "was amazed at his understanding and his answers."
5. His parents, on seeing him, evidently listened and watched from a distance instead of shrieking and embarrassing him publicly. "They were astonished" at what they saw, namely, his understanding and his answers.
6. His parents respected him, treated him gently, but they did not understand everything he was saying, even when he was speaking to them. His mother, though baffled by some of the details, treasured the episode in her heart.
7. He took his relationship to his parents seriously, respected them, and was obedient to them.
8. While he was free and responsible at twelve, he was still growing in wisdom, in stature, and in favor with God and everyone.

This material in Luke's gospel is all we have of Jesus' childhood, and we may assume it is given to us for profound reasons. One of them may be to show us the early age at which we might look toward transferring adult responsibilities in major proportions to our children.

Adult status as measured by a history of the transfer of work privileges or the transfer of responsibility to the child is most surprising. Koteskey traces the age at which maturity is recognized (in terms of ability to work and the legal age to marry) over a three-thousand-year span. Young men entered the work force at age twelve and were of an age to marry at fourteen for most of that three-thousand-year period almost until our own times. Those were the laws governing young men two hundred years ago in the United States. It was less complicated for young women, since for them marriage was the workplace. The age of entry as an adult woman was twelve as well for most of that time.

Look at Koteskey's time line[5] tracing the ages across Jewish, Roman, English, and American legal regulations for the last three thousand years:

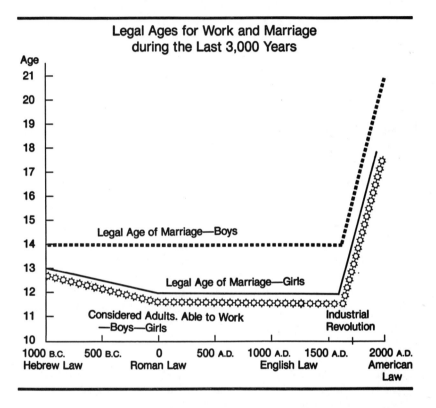

We need to ask what has caused this change in the age of adult status for young men and women. It would be easy to claim that life is too complex, or that they are too immature to make adult decisions. Indeed, children were abused and were forced to work in inhumane conditions in sweatshops, even coal mines. So child labor laws do represent our concern for the child's health and safety. Nevertheless teens have an astounding ability to make significantly complex decisions. All we need to do is watch children in an environment that favors their taking major responsibility for their own lives and their own use of time, for example, a Montessori school.

There is abundant evidence that the so-called problem of immaturity is more likely a result of our treatment of children and youth than the product of innate rebellion. Thus, if children and teens hold us in contempt, it is likely because they have the feelings of hostages toward captors.

Dare we admit it? Our young are kept at arm's length from employment and most meaningful activity not chiefly because they are incompetent, but because we do not want to share the rewards of the workplace. In the late twentieth century, while we still see the afterglow of the great family farms, it would be well to listen to the repertoire of heroic stories of teenagers at work, at management, at high productivity, and at the creative improvement of operations. The typical affirmation of many farmer-fathers was, "I'd trust my fourteen-year-old son with that piece of equipment or that operation more than I would anybody else I know who is two or three times his age!"

So here is the first half of the invention of adolescence. It is the tantalizing, frustrating postponement of responsibility, shutting out the human being from developing competence and making significant contributions to the human race and to the environment from approximately the age of thirteen to twenty. Labor laws prevent apprenticeships before the "legal age." A federal agency looks over the shoulders of today's farmers to be sure that unlicensed, "below age," relatives are not operating farm equipment. While we applaud every effort to prevent the exploitation of children, who will raise the urgent question: "Shall we deprive them of their sense of worth, their self-esteem, and put their impressive gifts and competence in cold storage for a decade? Shall we hold them hostage in their psychological development, call them 'boy' and 'girl' until they are twenty-five?" Then, after we have thus insulted them and devalued them, shall we be surprised that they hold us in contempt, that our values are regarded as rubbish, and that turning thirty is regarded as "going over the hill"? Or will we repent of our part in setting them up as prime targets in their arrested *child*hood to buy into what we now deplore as a play*boy* culture?

## The Secular Trend

While responsibility has quite suddenly disappeared for humans between the ages of about thirteen and twenty, an ironic opposite pattern has also emerged. Body height and sexual maturity have begun to develop earlier in the life cycle. It is the point at which these two trends cross that we can mark as the "invention of adolescence."

In the late 1960s, while I was knocking around Indiana University and studying under Boyd McCandless, William Lynch, and Shirley Engle, an image of adolescence began to form in my mind. I wish I could credit one of them with the diagram below, but I'm afraid it was a product of my doodling during seminars, gleaning tidbits of perceptual symbols and converting them into conceptual sketches. At any rate, Robbie and I were youth directors for the fairly complicated ministry with senior high young people at Winona Lake, Indiana's Free Methodist Headquarters Church. There was a sense in which the entire parade of generations of high school people moved through my mind when I studied adolescent development with McCandless, educational psychology with

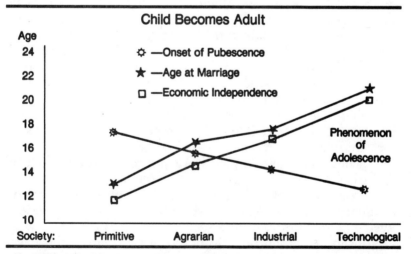

NOTE: This stylized drawing suggests how cultural variants of age at economic independence, age at marriage, and age at the onset of pubescence interplay to produce the phenomenon of adolescence in industrial and technological societies. It is ironic that pubescence strikes earliest in those cultures which hold off economic independence and marriage longest.

Lynch, and curriculum development with Engle. Here is the sketch.[6] I used it for at least fifteen years, apologizing that it was "stylized," that is, it was not based on research data but on cross-cultural descriptions of the teen years.

What I wanted people to see was that in any culture or in any family, we have "adolescence" whenever pubescence and sexual potency arrives before the child enters the workplace and is eligible for marriage. There appears to be a strange chemistry compounded of (a) adult vocation and economic independence, (b) legal right to marry as an adult, and (c) sexual, reproductive potency denoted by the onset of menarche in women and first ejaculation in men.

I will hypothesize that the magic moment for any human being occurs during the span of time when these three factors are "on line." If pubescence, marriage, and economic independence do not occur simultaneously, as in the Agrarian culture noted above, then we have potential stresses. It is critical that the cultural environment so respect the emerging adult as to guarantee a safe environment in which to allow a longer time for work, marriage, and sexual intimacy to form one profound moment of fulfillment. Only then will the integrity of the person be intact. If for any reason there is no job, marriage is denied, or sexual activity is trivialized, we may expect the complicated tasks of reconstruction. We will need to pick up the broken pieces of individual integrity and shattered self-esteem, not to mention the social consequences of the victims of sexual energy and productive energy gone awry. Adolescence, therefore, refers to the span of time during which the human being is "all dressed up with no place to go." Families and societies have an obligation to be looking for "landing spots" for these ripening humans.

It is here that Koteskey's historical research is most helpful and shocking. I had put him onto the scent of sexual development and even pointed him toward the collected literature cataloged as the "secular trend." I had, at that time, no idea what was secular about the secular trend, but it was a well-established research term to describe two things: the lower age at which sexual potency was received and the arrival of full body height. I wondered whether it was "secular" as opposed to "religious," but that made no sense. Eventually

I looked the word up in a good dictionary. Imagine my surprise to expand my vocabulary: "Secular: (1) occurring or observed but once in an age or century; (2) extending over or lasting for an indefinitely long period; opposite of 'periodical.'" So here it is: None of us will live long enough to see it come around again or to discern a pattern. It is moving without observable pattern, without cycle, without a clue where it will eventually go or whether it will return. The return of Halley's Comet is more predictable than is the pattern in this trend of the lowering age of sexual maturing.

A standard chart appears in many developmental psychology texts today showing the declining age at first menarche:

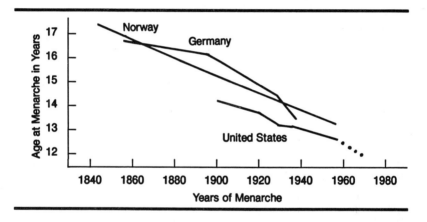

Elsewhere, I have summarized the likely causes of this changing pattern in sexual development.[7] Diet, climate, genetic pool, and light all have received attention and have appeared in a theoretical explanation for the phenomenon called the "secular trend." The reality of the decline, however, does not change because we can explain why it has occurred. Additionally, the point of this chapter is that our treasured young have been caught in the cross fire of a collision we have created in our culture, namely, the abolition of responsibility has collided with the earlier demands for sexual intimacy and for expression of full-spectrum affection. The pressure cooker of moral, physical, and spiritual crises set up our teens for a virtual explosion under the

sudden stresses we have created and continue largely to
ignore.

What Koteskey found in his historical search across Jewish,
Roman, British, and North American cultures is profoundly
simple. His documentation includes medical records, records
of marriages and births kept by churches for centuries, and
even choir records noting declining ages of boy sopranos.

> . . . Not a single one of the sixty-five studies done before 1880
> found an average age below fourteen and a half [for first menar-
> che]. Many were seventeen or more. By 1950, however, the aver-
> age was down to about twelve and a half or thirteen. . . .
>
> Puberty in men is not as obvious. . . . When Bach was choir-
> master at St. Thomas Church in Leipzig more than 200 years
> ago, boys often sang soprano until they were seventeen. Tenors
> and basses were men whose voices had already changed. Altos
> were those whose voices were changing. In 1744, Bach had ten
> altos, the youngest was fifteen and the oldest nineteen. Men's
> voices changed at about seventeen years of age then, but at about
> thirteen or fourteen now.[8]

Koteskey's diagram of this declining age of sexual maturity,
when placed on the three-thousand-year timeline, as you will
guess, "crosses over" our postponement of responsibility lines
for men and women. Look at the total picture of what happens
when the postponement of responsibility is laid over the rising
demand of the secular trend.

### A Priorities Check for Our Generation

With this historical picture we can begin to see, perhaps,
what we will never discover in our lifetimes if we imagine
that things have always been this way. If we can put adolescence in historical perspective, maybe we can do a priorities
check and ask whether we want to continue to drift into more
and more cultural, social, and even racial destruction. The
values may shake down like this:

1. Will our chief priority continue to be "economic advantage" and the protection of the workplace by inventing, expanding, and complicating certification through

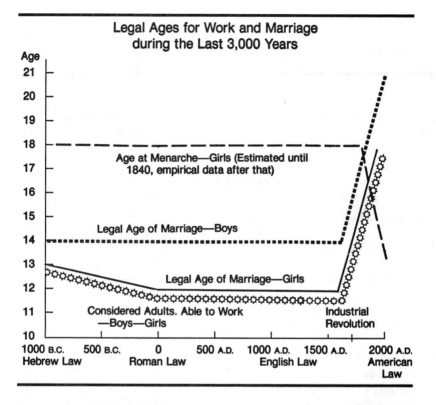

Legal Ages for Work and Marriage during the Last 3,000 Years

increasing education, internship, and high levels of schooling and degrees as prerequisite to achieving adult status?

2. Will our human resources, our young, continue to be pawns? Will they be devalued, turned off and away, not taken seriously or appreciated for the enormous intelligence and gifts they offer?

3. Will our legal and social party line continue to call for postponement of sexual expression until marriage, while our real agenda offers contraception, disease prevention, and abortion in a tacit endorsement of sexual irresponsibility?

If we settle for the status quo, we should not be surprised if the social order, the medical considerations, and the collapsing of marriages through desertion and divorce move on in the destructive pattern that characterizes the present age.[9] If we care about ourselves, our young, and our future, we obviously will look again at our values and make a new list of priorities:

1. Our young are our nonreplaceable resources and our only link to the future of the human family. Their health, emotional welfare, and lifelong effectiveness must take first priority.
2. Our economic resources and appetites are negotiable and can be downscaled to modify our patterns of extravagance and consumption. Our affluence can be made to serve the priority of protecting and developing our young generations—our nonreplaceable resources.
3. Our social and legal patterns can be brought in line with the common good and made to serve, protect, and sustain the vision of ourselves and our young—visions consistently characterized by exclusive, monogamous, full-fidelity marriages and families.

You and I, perhaps, are overly ambitious to hope to turn the tide of destructive trends in the whole of Western civilization. We are closer, however, to being able to bring constructive change when we know what is happening. All idols lose their power when we can call them by name. The "baal" of our time is adolescence, the invention of the rich and the powerful to enslave every generation of young. Many of us believe that the sacrifices that come by paying these dues are too costly to continue.

Counting Our Costs and Grieving Our Losses

Consider the price of supporting the monster of adolescence that we have unwittingly created.

1. Devaluing the young, damaging their sense of self-worth.
2. Frustrating their sexual energy and educating them through deception into trivializing their instincts for exclusive, monogamous, lifelong relationships.
3. Picking up the economic tab on all of our efforts to deal

with sexual promiscuity. We have thrown good money after bad by our failure to respect the complex nature of human sexuality with its intrinsic vision of wholeness and fidelity, and by our inept mangling of the best sexual resources of the young. Count the costs that bring us no constructive solution or direction: sex education, contraceptive education and services, abortion education and services, disease education and medical expenses related to sexually transmitted diseases, pregnancies, and abortions.

We are confronted with the task of abolishing adolescence. There are significant steps we can take now to get on with wholeness and health in families, in communities, and perhaps across whole cultures.

### Who Will Answer?

Whether or not we can turn the tide in one generation and find the priorities in values that can revive Western culture, it is clear that any family can cut its ties now with a sinking civilization. What is more, the influence of one person or of one family is hard to measure. It is a theme that leaves only a trace throughout the history of Israel, but the implications are electrifying.

God is represented occasionally in the prophets of Scripture as "looking for one person who could reach out, take to heart the tragedy and evil in the land." Often the cry comes back, "But I found no one." Eventually we see what God did for us in "one Man, Jesus," but the clues in the Old Testament suggest that God believed that one solitary person, one lonely family might have turned the tide by opening their hearts to "blot up" the hurt and pain of a broken society.

Edmund Burke is credited with memorable words:

> I am one.
> I am only one.
> But I am one.
> I cannot do everything
> But I can do something.
> What I can do, I will do.
> I am one.

At the very end of his astonishing study of clinical evil, *People of the Lie,* psychiatrist Scott Peck quotes the words of an old priest who had spent many years using the therapy of love to overcome evil:

> There are dozens of ways to deal with evil and several ways to conquer it. All of them are facets of the truth that the only ultimate way to conquer evil is to let it be smothered within a willing, living human being. When it is absorbed there like blood in a sponge or a spear into one's heart, it loses its power and goes no further.[10]

Peck goes on:

> The healing of evil—scientifically or otherwise—can be accomplished only by the love of individuals. A willing sacrifice is required. The individual healer must allow his or her own soul to become the battleground. He or she must sacrificially *absorb* the evil.[11]

Then, as a further example of the argument advanced first by the God of Israel in search of one person, Peck recalls the symbolic story from C. S. Lewis's Chronicles of Narnia where, in the first book, Aslan presents himself as the victim in behalf of all Narnia and is tied to the stone table and killed. Lewis explains: "When a willing victim who had committed no treachery was killed in a traitor's stead, the Table would crack and Death itself would start working backwards."[12]
Peck observes, then:

> I do not know how this occurs. But I know that it does. I know that good people can deliberately allow themselves to be pierced by the evil of others—to be broken thereby yet somehow not broken—to even be killed in some sense and yet still survive and not succumb. Whenever this happens there is a slight shift in the balance of power in the world.[13]

Who will answer? Likely some who themselves were wounded by adolescence? Parents are likely still to work out their own frustration on their children, consigning them to the same torture as they had to endure themselves, but not all will. If tenderness and love could work, we could change our families and we could perhaps start destruction working "backwards." If we could do that, then it would spell construction, and our grandchildren would rise up and thank us all.

### QUESTIONS PEOPLE ASK

*Q: I cannot believe that you are recommending that children be married at twelve! Can you imagine what kinds of problems that would create? Come on, now. Are you really recommending marriage as soon as pubescence hits?*

A: Not at all. Two more chapters follow in which I think you will be able to work out your family's positioning on the issues. Let me suggest, however, that I would rather marry off our children at twelve than to arm them with condoms at fourteen and send them out to the wolves of promiscuity, irresponsibility, and AIDS with every social signal that they are mere incompetent children until they finish military service or earn a master's degree. If those were your only choices, which would you choose? Fortunately, there are better options, but you rarely hear of them either in the churches or in the media these days.

*Q: Do you mean to suggest that as soon as a human being is sexually mature, ripened into an adult body, that he or she inevitably will become sexually active?*

A: No, but that is what we are being asked everywhere to believe. We are being brainwashed into thinking that everybody has a civil right to have whatever sex they want whenever they want it. History is littered with the wreckage of civilizations that went down with the same final cry. Surely this is not the road we want to travel. In this chapter I am only appealing that we begin with the facts of development and that we honestly look at those facts historically. I have a bold solution in Chapter 5 that allows us to regard early maturity as a blessing and not a curse; it calls for a supportive network around our young people to see them through to adult responsibility by building on that sexual frustration. So bear with me through these elementary observations and arguments.

# 4

# *What to Do? The Issues and Some Choices*

$\triangle$

Rolf and Luanne had dated since he had turned sixteen near the end of his sophomore year of high school. Luanne was a year younger. It was one of those friendships that attracted peer approval and gossip—"they are secretly engaged!"

Then, a month before his high school graduation, Rolf broke up with Luanne. It wasn't messy, just sudden and crisp—no second thoughts.

What none of us saw, Rolf told me later, was what had happened at home. Rolf's father and mother, impressive business and professional leaders in the community, had simply put it to him this way:

"Six months from now you'll be in Omaha at the university. Luanne will be here, still a senior in high school. You have four, maybe seven, years of schooling ahead of you. Who knows how much she will need? We aren't saying what you have to do, but we predict that your friendship with her will only tie her down for her senior year and will keep you from playing the field at the university. You know that marriage soon is out of the question; the day you are married is the day we stop helping you with schooling. Now, think it over."

"So," Rolf told me, "I thought it over, and I knew they were right. That's when I broke up with her."

In contrast, Jack's parents watched a whirlwind romance that had broken out at a summer convention. Then they watched, stunned, as Jack ended a high school romantic friendship with Vera in order to give full attention to Jill. They raised questions about how decisively he was acting. By Christmas, there was talk of transferring from his college to one where Jill would be enrolling after high school graduation, a school she could attend and continue to live at home. Following his extended visit to Jill's family over Christmas, Jack's parents sat him down:

"Look," his father said, "your mother and I have been watching this very closely. You are nineteen years old, and the two of you seem to have everything set but the wedding date."

"Oh, we've set that for four years from June!" he offered. "Jill will be finished with college and I will be in graduate school by then. We're engaged, but we don't have the money for a ring so we're not announcing it yet."

"If you are that sure of everything, why would you plan to wait four years? Why transfer to another school and ruin your grade point average by trying to carry on a romance every day and drag down your school work? Why don't the two of you get married next summer, instead?"

"I can't believe you said that!"

"We'll keep our support there to match whatever you can earn summers and on campus. And we'll do that until you get through your training. And if Jill's parents feel they can't help her after she is married, we'll do the same for her."

These two stories, poles apart as they are, represent the kinds of advice and leverage families tend to put on their young. There are other scenarios, too, and we will discuss them in this chapter. What I want you to feel as you work through the options in this chapter is that integrity parenting need not simply put on a blindfold and play a game of Russian roulette in guiding young adult children. Parents may identify and define priorities and arrange them to match exactly their values and beliefs.

## The Values We Prize

Here are some of those treasured, sometimes tightly held values:

1. The developing personalities of our child and the other person, with their need for integrity and intimacy.
2. The economic realities of launching a new household.
3. The social expectations of our families and our communities.

If the "to marry or to break up" issue could be resolved on one of these alone, we could patent the formula, but the personal-social-economic mix is always complicated. Let's look at the value issues, above, in reverse order so as to get a first reading and focus on what they may stand for.

*Social values.* By this category I mean to cluster together two sorts of things. First, you can make all decisions based on what you imagine other people think. Second, I mean to include the popular social folklore, often accepted as truth on social matters by writers and counselors of the young.

Those guidelines today, for example, show up in popular statements that ring with such "truth" that they are regarded as common sense. Among these popular gospels is the often-repeated warning that early marriages end in divorce. They go on to recommend that "experienced" partners make better husbands and wives. Psychological maturity, they tout, tends to arrive at around age thirty for most people, and most people are poor marriage risks before that age. Those values undergird the sex therapists you tend to hear on television, the values of popular talk shows, and virtually the entire entertainment industry.

"What other people think" brings popular folklore down to main street. Early marriage is a scandal in a small community. The lingering finger points suspiciously: "Count the months until the first baby!" Or worse, "Are they so dumb they didn't think of getting an abortion? What a pity the young think they have to be married to have sex."

What we see in the social values issue is that we are always at the mercy of popular opinion. Popular opinion, however, often serves false gods. Social values, regrettably, frequently rest on the lowest possible common denominator. They assume everybody is evil and that the smart people are the ones who leave no "tracks." "Goodness" is thus equated with being "smart." Therefore, hide the lack of integrity in your young by insisting that they use the services of Planned Parenthood or the family physician to get themselves fixed against a pregnancy, or at the worst, head for the abortion clinic and keep the secret off the streets.

*Economic values.* Again the folklore has a clear mandate on parents. "Kids are your responsibility until they are through school, but after they are married, they are on their own!" In some families and some communities, the economic sword is used to sever the umbilical cord to family resources on high school graduation day. In such cases, the young typically join the Army or otherwise get out of the house and off to some craft or other to survive alone. In either case, these young adults are victims of foreclosure of the family system. Until our own time, no other culture in the history of the world dropped its young off cold into adult responsibilities without inheritance, property, dowry, craft, or support from the launching households. Our devaluing of our young by this inhumane treatment will stand in human history as a low point in our culture. No doubt this will be described in detail by sociologists and historians when they write of the decline of Western civilization.

*Personal values.* How do we measure the value of one person? How much are two people worth? What would you pay if you could "risk proof" your children against sexual promiscuity? Against infidelity in marriage? Against dependency on alcohol or on drugs? Against abusing your grandchildren? If you found a way to thus form healthy children and launch responsible young adults, would you find a way to modify your family life patterns and your child-rearing strategies? Would you be bold enough to raise your children contrary to accepted folklore and in full view of relatives and friends who have bought into the values of popular culture? Would you find a way to modify your spending habits and to marshal the resources of the entire household to foot the economic bill?

It is my thesis throughout this book that the value of persons always wins—hands down. There is no competition. It is also my thesis that social values ought to be held in suspicion most of all. None of us will live long enough to discover the origins of our folklore, but there is a central tendency for social pressure to be destructive, to devalue persons, and to weigh down the young. Integrity parenting always is committed to the value of the young and to discipline and care that predicts for maturity and responsibility. It involves intimate communication and caring that is expressed in a thousand ways, including words.

I hold, conversely, that when social expectations or economic issues determine our patterns in parenting, we have succumbed to the voices that turn our children into mere objects. We have taken an instrumental approach to child-rearing and launching. We have treated our children as pawns, used them as we pleased, to win for ourselves the social approval or financial successes we need; we have reduced our young to chattel. At some level we could call this type of parenting a "functional approach." In this instrumental parenting, children are used as objects for display, they are trained, tutored, and coached to succeed *for us* and not for their own good. Parenting today has bought heavily into this functional pattern of child-rearing and launching.

Look at some of the options from which today's family chooses to deal with emerging adult issues in the lives of their young. We will examine a set of options that leads to the separation of sexual activity from adult responsibilities. Then I want you to evaluate the options that keep adult responsibilities locked together, linking sexual intimacy with vocational and marital responsibilities.

## Beyond Freedom and Dignity

I use B. F. Skinner's book title[1] for this section with some ambivalence. He offers a glimpse at a world in which everybody does what they are programmed to do by behavioristic training. Such a world, he says, is one where conscience is not needed because no one is responsible for individual behavior. The popular options available to us as parents do not include a strictly behavioristic model such as Skinner envisioned. Instead, the set of permissive models tends to rest on a premise very similar to Skinner's, namely, that young people will be young people—they will only do what comes naturally. If that were true, then of course they are not responsible for their actions—a point of view many parents want to embrace. If, however, they are only doing what comes naturally and cannot do otherwise, then Skinner is right—they are also beyond freedom. The young cannot not behave as they do.

Among the popular models of child-launching that buy into the permissive, do-what-feels-good perspective, I want to describe Erik Erikson's understanding of the psychosocial moratorium as a foundation to help understand the more common parenting models of precocious adolescence programming and safe-sex education.

*Psychosocial moratorium.* Put at its simplest level, Erikson described what he found Americans were doing with their teenage children. Knowing, as he did, the eager search for identity that is common to middle teen years, Erikson would never have invented the psychosocial moratorium. Indeed, it represents an issue over which he and all of us may properly grieve.

The psychosocial moratorium refers to the damage we do to normal psychological development and social responsibility of young adults between approximately thirteen and twenty-five. This moratorium—shutting down—of psychological development means the young adult forfeits the dream of a life and vocation with meaning. The moratorium requires that they forfeit that vision for at least twelve years, and give up on the hope of developing a genuine adult relationship that can lead to legally and socially approved marriage.

When we deny children their full share of responsibility for choices and behavior, for whatever motive, we tend to shield them from adulthood as well. In the next chapter we will look at the role of pain as a catalyst for maturing. Even though we tell ourselves that we want to shield our children from pain, we have neglected to admit that simultaneously we have denied them their human inheritance as well. That is, however, only one side of the moratorium. There is a social cost as well.

Society pays a high price, too. The psychosocial moratorium requires that the whole culture shut down its expectations that this very adult-looking person will, in fact, behave in responsible ways. On the one hand, society agrees to postpone the normal age at which a person may be employed. This part of the moratorium takes the form of labor laws that prohibit the young adult from working before the age of sixteen or eighteen. Then society invents credentialing through college and university programs, quite apart from the fact that the credentials tend to have mixed reviews as to their effectiveness in preparing our young for adult responsibilities, much less for specific professions. Then, to be sure that there is something for everybody, we appeal to the poor who cannot get to college (even with enormous public underwriting) and invite them to join the Army, Navy, Air Force, or Marines during the moratorium years. Both college and military service tend to put the parents at ease because whatever irresponsibility children are involved in, they are doing it someplace else and not embarrassing the parents. What we don't know doesn't hurt us. Besides, society adjusts its court system so that they will be tried and judged as though they were children, at least until age eighteen.

On the other hand, society picks up the tab for the entertainment of these socially arrested moratorium kids. The life process has stalled in the teen moratorium and it calls for parents, communities, churches—for all of us—to underwrite what amounts to a ten- to twelve-year party. "What is college?" one wag asked, then answered: "A four-year loaf on father's dough."

*Precocious programming.* It would be one thing to arrest the developmental calendar of our young (especially if we retained the environment of childhood in which their play might be supervised and the consequences kept at the childhood level). It is quite another, however, when parents have so instrumentalized their kids that they want to guarantee them the full rights and privileges of adult fun and pleasure with none of the responsibilities. Check the parking lot of any high school when the day ends and watch the playboy and playgirl children rev up their toys—furnished either by sympathetic parents who pity them in their locked-up moratorium and therefore want to make life tolerable in the playpen, or by harassed parents who are victims of social pressure and do not want their child rejected because there is no sports car in the teen's garage. Some of the playpen equipment is likely milked out of parental largess simply from the parents' fondness for watching the sexual energy of their young being splayed against the winds of youth.

David Elkind and others have cried out against the foreclosure of childhood.[2] Kindergarten and elementary school children find themselves now embroiled in "king and queen" contests, in "proms" and dances, and in "dating." Add to these social programs the silent killer of childhood—cable television—whose unrestricted programming haunts the latchkey houses where children are seduced into sexually stimulating and addicting material well ahead of their already lowered age of pubescence. We are appalled at the statistics which suggest that large numbers of high school students are sexually active. Yet we often feel intimidated into accepting that this is the way teenagers are and the way things are. When we do that, we are fulfilling Skinner's prophecy: We and our children are beyond freedom and dignity.

*Safe-sex advice.* Many parents are afraid and desperate. Others seem motivated by their own erotica as they fantasize about their teenagers' sexual possibilities. These seductive parents seem intent on pushing their children into sexual action so that their voyeurism will be rewarded with pornographic images of illicit and experimental young sex. Today's young adults are full of documentation about parental seduction through suggestion, innuendo, accusation, and the availability of paraphernalia for safe sex. The seduction extends to arranged weekends with unlimited privacy and the luxury of beach condos or vacant homes while parents are away.

With the arrival of new sexually transmitted diseases, the array of safe sex equipment may now be seen regularly in all our living rooms via television. The clear signal here is that everybody is doing it so it is important to do it safely. If this is true, if the young are helpless victims of their hormones and their sexuality, then we are indeed living in Skinner's world beyond freedom and dignity.

*Toward Freedom and Dignity, Through Responsibility*

It would be hard to identify a perspective to which I am more opposed than that of Skinnerian determinism with its forfeiture of dignity and freedom. So here let me simply turn his thesis on its head and offer choices at the opposite end of the spectrum. The popular culture in which we live is buying into its own form of passive determinism, wringing its hands occasionally to deplore the collapse of moral vision. Popular sociologists and psychologists tell us that the human race is changing, thus calling us to roll with the tide. Some of us, however, have another perspective. We are quite sure there are alternative choices that are consistent with something that never changes. We suspect that there is a core of integrity at the center of every human being which, if nurtured, can rise to greatness and full responsibility. Although we are not sure that anything good can come from pretending the core is not there, we suspect that such neglect leads to destructive human experiences, perhaps to death. Look at some choices that make for life and hope and stability. As is true in any arena at all, freedom comes only to those who are responsible.

*Protective isolation.* We might call them enclaves of safety—I refer first of all to those attempts by which a family or a group of families pulls down the curtains to the outside world in an effort to insulate their young from the popular culture. We have classical communities that have frozen the culture of a bygone day, have rejected electricity and the internal combustion engine in an effort to establish an environment in which to impart their unique identity to future generations. Typically, in my part of the world during childhood, the children of such a community were taken out of public school and put to work on the farm or at some other craft at about age twelve. It seemed a tragedy to me in many ways, but I noted that they did maintain a clear and identifiable subculture with its own value system nicely passed along.

Some families have abolished television and radio and popular sounds from the music charts in an effort to prevent the culture's values from bombarding them and their young.

Many of these have resorted to home schooling in order to nurture their values, traditions, and beliefs. In some communities similar families or congregations have banded together to organize private alternative schools, largely for the purpose of controlling cultural programming. These groups may on the surface look like God's "frozen few." Although their successes may be isolated instances in shutting out the corrupting environment, they may turn out to be the real futurists in our society.

We should realize that they value their children as persons and not as objects. We will want to ask whether they are effective in confronting the popular culture and are not merely maintaining parallel, privately funded schooling that expresses the same sexual values as the culture at large. A look at their pageantry, their silence about sexuality in general and about sexual integrity in particular, will give us clues. We also want to see whether they are proactive and constructive or whether they are simply reactive and negative toward all of life. We will want to observe how they deal with failure, with children who rebel or successfully leave the enclave in search of a life outside. We will expect them to resist social pressures, at least those from outsiders, but we will want to see how they deal with the economics of launching children, with supporting the critical events of finding a vocation and entering marriage on a schedule that realistically takes into account their developing sexuality.

*Participative immunity.* Consider what a family might choose as its parenting strategy if it regarded its young as its treasured, nonreplaceable gifts, and if they concluded that they must immunize their children against the values of an alien environment while living in it. How would they regard their children if they saw them as unique, as too valuable on which to perform some great social experiment? What would their support and their discipline look like? If you could eavesdrop on them, what would they talk about? How might they form a bonded conspiracy to resist the world, the flesh, and the devil? How would they regard the social fads and pressures that move through the generations? What would their financial priorities be? What would family life look like if parents were not using their children and children were not inclined to use their parents?

What we might expect to see would be an intergenerational solidarity that resists social pressure, that regards economic assets as community property, and an affection holding this sense of respect in place. It is only fair to ask the same hard questions of them: How do they deal with failure, with the loss of some treasured son, daughter, father, or mother who leaves for the far country of the popular culture and its values? If they shun or otherwise punish those who leave, then they are likely holding an instrumental view of persons. Only the authority center has changed. We will want to see how they handle the economic needs of their generations, and we will be particularly attentive to their ways of synchronizing vocation, marriage, and the sexual energy that now arrives so early.

Indeed this book will be devoted to tracing and developing the best information we have on this approach to marriage, parenting, and the family. Its thesis is simple: We live in a troubled world, but we belong to each other. We will live in honesty, calling destructive trends and practices by name and helping one another to identify both old and new threats to everything that makes for health and life. We know that all of us live at risk, but we are building relationships that hold us steady in the face of the siren song of the world, the flesh, and the devil. We are, however, never arrogant. We always have an eye out for other people who are ready to find their way out of the destructive forces at work everywhere. So we are evangelists in some radical sense of constantly being people of good news and hope.

I have outlined in this chapter the alternatives that face us as we look at the explosive timing of the emerging young adult agenda: the need for vocation, for marriage, and for harnessing the awakening sexual energy of pubescence. The spectrum that unfolds here is only a painting. The facts are always more complicated. The general patterns are visible on any day in your town and mine. I want you next to turn to look at the adolescent crucible and the role of pain in forming the character of mature human beings anywhere, anytime.

## QUESTIONS PEOPLE ASK

*Q: I really hoped you would tell us how to guarantee that our kids would turn out well. There seems so much risk in all the alternatives. Can't you give us more assurance than this?*

A: I doubt that you are willing to take the whole package that comes with a guarantee. If we could guarantee outcomes, then we would deny both the Creation and our present respect for the value of persons. God took the first parental risk. So with that precedent we do not have to feel that the risks are too great. We have the advantage, living as we do in the late twentieth century, of being able to look at family life and at some of the predictable consequences of styles of family discipline and decision making. In later chapters we will see that we can predict very well that position "A" leads in most cases to consequence "A." So I think all of us are more comfortable with predicting than we would be with guaranteeing at the expense of altering the Creation's commitment to respect by which persons freely choose, even though the consequences are destructive. Determinism comes at a very high price, and God did not want us locked into guarantees or fixed outcomes.

*Q: I really object to the idea that parents should support their married children. I surely do not want my teenager reading this chapter. She would get ideas with which I couldn't cope and by which I don't intend to live.*

A: We do have a nice deal going for us in the modern era: We can dangle our children over economic ruin in exchange for their good behavior, or at least the appearances of good behavior. If you had to choose between the following options, which would you be willing to choose: (1) See your daughter move in with her boyfriend right after high school graduation? (2) See her date around and sleep around secretly, establishing promiscuity as her lifestyle for the next thirty years? (3) Support her marriage and her education based on the integrity you find in both children as they generate visions of marital intimacy combined with the pursuit of high vocational goals?

Those are the choices parents are making every week, and you are very likely to be confronted with taking a position on the issues included here. I really do hope she discusses the options before she senses your rigidity and shocks you into accepting her freedom to choose as she moves in and out of brief encounters of the promiscuous sort.

# 5

# *Pain:  Catalyst for Maturity?*

△

Paul and Beth came into our lives through a crossover of professional services. I found myself taking bids on a job, and Paul was a contractor. He not only won the bid but got our friendship besides. Over the next two years we moved socially back and forth several times, then the two of them dropped the bomb. They were on the verge of divorce. Beth showed up at our house with severe facial bruises. We cared so much about them that we pulled Paul immediately into the scene. They were able to keep the marriage, but in the process of reconciliation the story came out, first from one then the other. Most of the stories were told to us privately. Beth had three lovers in late high school and college years. Paul became sexually active during high school, the first a long-term relationship that, he said, "we both were sure would lead to marriage." It lasted only two years after they started the sexual involvement, and they had been going together since they were in junior high.

"Whatever happened to her?" I asked, intuitively worrying about what effects the high school sexual experience might have left on her.

"Nothing good. She really came apart when we broke up—

went really crazy. That was fifteen years ago, and she has been sleeping around ever since."

"What about you?"

"Every woman I ever looked at after that I took to bed. Beth doesn't know it, but it still is going on with me. I just can't seem to stop it."

Now, twenty years later, Beth and Paul have long since been divorced. Their children carried the marks of the troubled home into high school and were apparently easy prey to sex and drugs. Beth has remarried and appears to be moderately stable, although she is astonishingly overweight. It is a problem she blames on how she feels about herself. Paul continues his work as a competent contractor; he has developed arthritis and suffers a great deal. He would probably be called a workaholic by any measure, but, as he says, "There's nobody at home, so why go home?"

"I gave it all to Jesus," he told me about five years ago when we bumped into each other at a convention. "I have plenty of time to read the Bible. I wish I had taken the time when I was about twelve or fifteen. I'd never have been alone at this time of life if I had my head on straight then."

In a very different painful story, Del found himself single at twenty-five and finished with his graduate work. He found an apartment he could afford on the outskirts of Detroit. He had channeled his interest in girls mostly into being a star athlete in high school and enjoying their attention. Off to a Christian college, he dated occasionally but held the few special women at a distance that guaranteed "nothing would happen, because I knew I had a long road ahead." That distance pattern became his standard operating procedure, and he earned a reputation for being casual and temporary.

Now that training was behind him, Del was ready for romance. His emotions, at twenty-five, had a long-term bridle keeping them under control. His address book was bulging with the names and phone numbers of women with whom he had one or a dozen dates, all carefully calculated to go nowhere. He was continuing to add names to the list.

Del was on a continuous search for the dream woman. He wondered why he could not suddenly find that one exclusive relationship about which he dreamed. One day he did a

bold thing. While walking through a shopping mall in suburban Detroit, he spotted a stunning woman. He courageously
stepped inside the women's apparel shop and asked a ma-
tronly looking saleswoman whether the younger woman was
married. Del learned that Judy was, indeed, eligible. The
older woman called Judy to the scene, embarrassing Del, and
the introduction was executed. Judy, too, had dated around—
and more. He took her to church and found she evoked the
approval of his friends there. She was a bit uneasy finding him
quite active in leadership roles both in the program and in the
spirit of his church. She may have felt guilty, too, at his deep
religious commitment partly because of her past promiscuity.
Del and Judy found an impressive magic in their relationship,
and he thought a heavenly marriage might be just around the
corner. Then, one night in her apartment as he thought it was
time to leave she put it to him.

"I want you in bed. Now. Tonight."

"I've never been to bed with anybody, and I won't be until
I'm married to her."

"But I adore your body. You make me really nervous in
almost everything else—your job and your religion and your
church—but I really love your body."

Del was devastated. "I'm sorry you don't like the things I
have worked hard to be and to do. I trained for my job, and
I have worked hard to be good at it. The stuff about church
and Jesus—I have to take responsibility for all of that. I intentionally made them my priorities. Those are the things you
don't like very much. The only thing you like is something
that isn't mine. My body is rented. I'm responsible for it, but I
didn't choose it. God gave it to me. So I can't give it away."

Stepping out into the night, Del found himself still alone.

These two swatches of pain, miles apart as they are, represent the sort of agony that comes with sexual choices and sexual behavior. Most often those choices and experiences come
to us in the years between thirteen and thirty. Paul and Beth
have telltale marks of the pain in their bodies. Some are the
marks of normal aging, of course, but the desperately low
sense of self-esteem has marked Paul with several decades
of alcohol dependency with its debilitating marks on his
digestive and circulatory systems. Beth is still overweight, a

compulsive eater. She has chosen clothing styles that mask her unsightly thighs and legs. They seem prematurely old. Paul and Beth have wisdom that came late, but they have a prospect of becoming gentle, safe, and helpful in giving us a perspective on what matters most.

Del's suffering is still going on. His loneliness as he now enters his thirties is sometimes unbearable. His coaching career has served as a magnet to pull scores of young men and women toward integrity in all of life. He has credibility as an advocate of self-discipline, and his life is an open book to the young who flock around him.

Some patterns would emerge if we were to examine the variations in pain among the three people we have described here. Paul and Beth both thought they were "home free" in their early sexual adventures. "Everybody's doing it." "It's fun." "Be cool." These were the attitudes. For them, the pain came later. They were aware early that breakups felt terrible. Their visions exploded. There would always be other relationships, and as they made it into the fast lane, there was excitement simply in the high-speed chases and the fast switches in partners.

The pain started getting them down when they realized they were out of control. Their adult lives were shattered at some deeper, inner level they couldn't seem to fix. The alcohol, food, and tranquilizers deadened the pain and allowed them to maintain the appearances of a family, a marriage, and a civilized household. Paul and Beth's pain came as a consequence, and consequences never are quite predictable.

Del has been suffering since he was thirteen. Early sexual maturity plagued him with desire. He gritted his teeth, kept his distance, designed a speed control on his reach for intimacy, and now finds that the most attractive women in his world tend to be sexually promiscuous and aggressively so. He feels sure that God will answer his prayers for a gracious and good woman, but he is realistic in seeing the improbability of finding that match easily. He prays a lot about it, sometimes crying out to God in impatience and frustration. Del's pain is coming out of chosen self-discipline. The discipline is quite predictable. He has not scattered pain through other people's lives, and he can live with the continuing pain of self-discipline as long as that is necessary. He has no need for alcohol or medication to give him a good night's sleep—or to let him deal with his inner conscience. He looks ten years younger than his calendar age.

### Crucible: Is There Life after Pubescence?[1]

Let me take you back to the stylized drawing that highlighted the invention of adolescence. I want you to look at the expanding strain placed on any effort to hold together the three markers: vocational entry, legal marriage, and sexual maturity. I have drawn loops to enclose the three and have noted the number of years the tension must be sustained if personal integrity is developed in the emerging adult.

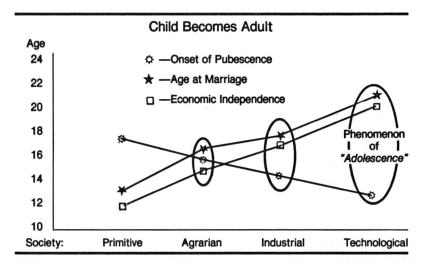

There is a simple pattern at work in history, as we noted in the last chapter. It is this: as human communities became more complex, children were gradually shut out from adult responsibilities. Schools were invented and expanded, and more and more training programs were developed to prepare them for responsibilities in technological cultures. The big surprise in all this is that under those same cultural conditions, and only under high-tech stresses, sexual development moved in the opposite direction—pubescence arrives earlier and earlier.

It would be easy to conclude that God made a mistake in creating humans to torment them out of their minds with being "all dressed up with no place to go." I want to offer another perspective. It is this: the stressing of sexual maturity against postponed privileges and responsibilities is essential to produce moral giants whose wisdom is needed to sustain human values and to protect the exploding human race with its capabilities of annihilating itself with its technological inventions. Let's demonstrate that thesis by looking at each of the four conditions in the diagram above and asking what sort of responsibilities humans would have in each of the cultures and what the potential stresses are in their developmental experience.

## When Sexual Maturity Follows Adult Status

You can see as you examine the four conditions represented on the chart that primitive cultures seem to anticipate adulthood and value it for the child. Primitive peoples tend to live in significant isolation from outside cultures and to have little contact or communication with them. They have highly developed language and oral traditions and stories, but rarely has their language been reduced to writing. Their moral code is minimal but fixed. They have little energy to spend caring for irregular behavior in the community, so the death penalty is common for infractions of community standards.

Primitive cultures tend to have elaborate rites of passage in which the boys are initiated and made into warriors or hunters while we would still think of them as boys. This often occurs around the age of twelve. Age twelve remains in our ages of confirmation, Bar Mitzvah, and admission into believer's baptism. Perhaps it is a carryover from the days when we took children seriously as adults long before sexual maturity arrived.

In addition to the adult status of vocation as a hunter or a warrior, the boy is typically ready for an arranged marriage. The arranging, of course, involves the parents, and the criteria tend to be based on tribal status and economic factors. The boy in a patrilineal culture continues the family name and fortune, so it is of no small significance how his bride is chosen.

In primitive cultures the girl will be received into the adult vocation, sometimes also with a rite of passage, although these rarely are as elaborate as those for boys. The girl who is ready for womanly work as defined in the culture is also an object of attention. She has value. There will often be a bride price. This is usually based on her general desirability as a bride and on her status and family wealth. In a matrilineal culture, it is typically the bride's mother who can delay this prepubescent wedding, sometimes for a few months or years, until she is granted the price for which she is bargaining. A Kipsigese mother in Kenya today, for example, may hold out until she gets thirty cows for the daughter she is releasing as a bride. All of this sets the stage for vocation and marriage to have occurred ahead of the awakening surge of sexual energy that comes with sexual ripening at pubescence.

For our purposes it will be important to do some observing and predicting. Since the issues are economic and social, the moral dimensions of taking responsibility for surging sexual desires are removed. If moral reasoning and the potential consequences of sexual failure are removed, we can predict that moral reasoning may remain at a relatively simple problem-solving level. We may have here an insight into the differences in moral perception and reasoning that are observed and measured across cultural levels. Justice remains among primitive people largely a matter of reciprocity, of dealing out what one has received: an eye for an eye, a tooth for a tooth.[2]

### Simultaneous Line Up: No Crucible

The agrarian culture is made up of that sample of human communities that exists in remote rural areas and manages to remain independent of the outside world. These may be fixed-place peoples or nomadic, following their herds of domestic animals. They tend to have developed written language, to be aware of other cultures, and to retain distinct identity away from them. In modern times we have witnessed the Amish and some Old Order Mennonite communities that remind us how an agrarian people can hold themselves distinct from a dominant culture into which they have stumbled. There are similarities between the early Puritans who escaped to America and today's agrarian cultures. In both cases the community escaped an industrial culture and seemed to revert to agrarianism out of necessity: they had to survive, and they were locked into the soil and into their own limited resources.

In such agrarian cultures as these, the community has an enormous interest in their future as an isolated value community. In my boyhood, we expected the Old Order Mennonite boys to leave school at about age thirteen, just as pubescence was hitting. When the beard appeared, they must be about manly things, and marriage and parenthood were profoundly rewarding trophies held out before those young men. Their belief system was nicely synchronized with their emerging sexual energy.

In a similar way, the Puritans can easily be documented as wishing to guarantee that their children would not be overly tempted as their sexual maturity appeared. Marriage was to be the automatic solution to the otherwise tormenting frustration of "being all dressed up with no place to go." We saw in chapter 3 that early American ages for vocation and marriage were twelve to fourteen years. These ages were brought right out of emerging industrial England where child labor ran the factories. They were sustained until the last century, largely due to the practical considerations of the newly planted agrarian colonies. Families were assertive in monitoring courting behavior, providing a chaperone, and anxiously avoiding opportunities for sexual contact among the unmarried.

As the age at marriage was slowly rising, more and more rigorous laws appeared on the books to protect minors from sexual activity. Laws about statutory rape and contributing to the delinquency of a minor stand on the books, rarely cited today, but they are reminders that the agrarian way of handling emerging sexual energy has faded. Under that vision, children were granted adult status with the simultaneous alignment of vocation, marriage, and the arrival of full body height and physical evidences of sexual maturity.

When these three factors line up, we see a profile of moral reasoning: a high sense of responsibility; respect for the authorities that orchestrate job, sex, and marriage; and patterns of adherence to law and to decisions of other authoritative decision-makers and a willingness to wait to become a decision-maker through seniority. These cultures tend to hold to deep traditions, to be either patriarchal or matriarchal, and to resist change with some sense that the order would collapse if any part were modified.

I take the position that the alignment of the three adult maturity factors strongly predicts that moral reasoning is locked into maintaining existing values and structures. The security of the system links with the fairly simple moral choices that are necessary to combine to produce a fresh generation which drops out of the larger culture at just the time their emerging sexual maturing is being affirmed. These youth tend to celebrate the closed culture to the tune of their awakening adult sexuality and to become the protectors of the closed subculture that has produced and shaped them, but there are exceptions.

### Crucible as Pain through Curbing of Desire

I want you to look now at the stress that begins to build in what I have labeled as industrial cultures. It virtually explodes under the tensions of the technological culture. Industrial cultures are those that have widened their scope from mere agrarian dependency on the soil. They have established communication and heavy use of language across cultural lines, but they are fiercely independent of other cultures for their survival. They take pride that "made in this country" means the rest of the world could disappear and they would survive. You can see that the industrial culture's view of the outer world is different from that of the agrarian. There the order was preserved by constructing fences: withdrawal, isolation, unique lifestyle, and often unique garb, language, and rituals. Such people were almost at war against the encroachment of outer world cultures. In the industrial culture, however, there is awareness of the outer world, significant imitation of it, competition with it, and an economic defense against becoming in any way dependent on other cultures.

Industrial cultures are noted for a sense of pride in their identity, for making a place for their own in factories, and for getting ahead of other competitor cultures. A historian might throw light on motivations for wars in the last two hundred years by citing this competition-within-isolation mixture. Indeed military service has become, for many of them, the first male vocation, and sexual energy is approved only after that service, unless, of course, they are involved in a military action (in which rape and exploitation of the victim women is applauded). Once in the workplace, marriage tends to come earlier than in the technological culture.

The technological culture is a logical extension of the trends we have seen. Now sexual maturity arrives nearly ten years ahead of the granting of adult status through vocation and marriage, as we say, "without parental consent." I want to discuss both of these cultures together because they give us the conditions under which enormous stresses are released between sexual energy and the social restrictions that the emerging adult feels in the marketplace and in traditional expectations for marriage responsibilities.

The stresses are first set off by earlier sexual potency. This is accompanied by earlier full body height and adult appearance. Yet at the same time that sexual energy is emerging earlier, we have moved the goal posts of adult vocation and marriage further back. If this goal movement had been done simply to tantalize the young, we could make a case for the prosecution of the culture for torture. A very different reason for postponing adult status, however, is actually given: we have assumed that a child is incompetent to make decisions needed in the complicated culture in which we live and move. We have assumed that a child needs skills with which to cope and to contribute to the economic growth of the complex marketplace.

Thus we have developed, invented, and proliferated training programs. We have attached high prices to the educational programs. We have essentially pulled the rug out from under the emerging adults making them at the same time economically on their own, while they, by our standards, remain unqualified to support themselves. Parents who in other cultures would have been attentive to dowry and bride price, plus setting up the new family in business, today withhold the launching expense totally or limit it to helping out with college unless youth do something stupid like getting married.

Note that this frustration of vocation-economic support sends a potential torpedo into the fragile eggshell that is already stretched to a breaking point between early sexual energy and later marriage. I want to argue that the sex-marriage tension is sufficient to produce moral reasoning giants alone without the harassment of rattling money in the face of the still-dependent adult who is shut out of the marketplace without more and more training.

At any rate, these stresses (that begin to appear in the industrial culture and which all but explode in the technological culture) create a sufficient scenario for the maximum development of moral reasoning power. This stress may produce two very different effects, and I want to discuss those separately. Here it is enough to say that either of the two options may lead to the highest moral sensitivity of which humans are capable. Pain seems to set the scene in which every option has to be explored, every perspective taken, and every decision defended from the widest possible argument. These painful and painstaking decision processes and the consequences of those decisions provide the moral agenda in which giants may emerge. It is ironic, but not surprising, that humans are so created that their capacity for highest moral reasoning is linked with such variable cultural conditions. *It is as if we are built with moral hardware already installed, but it can be activated only to the moral reasoning level necessary to support the complexity of the ethical dilemmas that present themselves in the prevailing culture.*

Industrial and technological cultures pose increasingly complex moral problems. For example, what is the role of environment for predicting irregular behavior? The older simple rules that led to execution for theft were suited for maintenance of a relatively uncomplicated culture with limited ways of dealing with irregular behavior and crimes. Complex cultures find ways of diagnosing, treating, and incarcerating individuals who revolt against their societies— ways of postponing the death sentence with a view to solving problems in humane ways. We may groan and be angered that delays in justice are counterproductive, but they are signs that moral reasoning is engaging many more ways of assigning guilt and accountability.

So today, when moral judgments are mushrooming, our young have a curriculum for moral excellence built into their natural environments. Many of them will be morally deformed, imbecilic, and incompetent, unable to serve us well. Others, however, will excel and exceed our own moral sensitivity and wisdom. God knows we need them—we need them now.

## The Pain of Chastity

Keep your eye on the diagram to note the stretch in time between sexual maturity and marriage. We are looking for our supposed moral reasoning agenda that creates the conditions which form the higher reaches of sensitivity to truth and justice and mercy.

We can count on a universal human expectation that sexual activity belongs within one exclusive lifelong relationship.[3] This means that as the time begins to stretch out, a moral pressure cooker begins to heat up for the emerging adult. The pressure points revolve around key issues, each of them significantly contributing to the need to reason through the issues:

1. Feelings of frustration and confusion: Did God make a mistake? I'm ready for lifelong bonding, but am I old enough? Is there something wrong with me? Am I deformed—am I oversexed?
2. Feelings of self-blame and shame: Something's wrong with me because I'm preoccupied with sexual yearning. People would not respect me if they knew how sexually motivated I am.
3. Feelings of loneliness and estrangement. There is a tendency to want to reach out and touch someone, but there is no way to make the gestures that lead to intimacy without lying, merely leading up to promises that cannot be kept.

4. All of these are inflamed or aggravated by feelings that the pain of abstinence may not be worth it, that "If I cannot live up to my ideals, I must be a failure, so I might as well cave in and go with the flow." On the other hand, for those who hold out, abstinence leads either to a feeling of social isolation or contributes to an enormous sense of personal strength.

5. Celibacy (by which I mean living the life of sexual integrity that abstains from all sexual contact) becomes the only morally sound way of life for emerging adults in an industrial or technological culture. With this kind of moral stress building over time, it is an understatement to assert that *sexual maturity combines with postponed vocation and marriage to constitute a powerful curriculum to test and develop a high competency of moral reasoning and moral courage.* Indeed both the vocation of celibacy (which may be entered into voluntarily as a moral covenant) and the involuntary call to celibacy (which may face the spouse of a sexually incompetent mate) represent acid tests of moral strength. Our sexuality is such a central feature of our personhood, and we have such a deep hunger for intimate affirmation through sharing, that only the strongest of disciplines can sustain celibacy.

## The Pain of Moral Failure

We sometimes object that the word "moral" is so closely linked to sexual themes. It may be that we first encounter the rigors of moral tension in the sexual arena, so our minds go to our primal experience. Two factors combine to establish healthy genital contact: (1) personal integrity (being a truthful person known for consistency and open honesty in all relationships) and (2) the healthy ability to reach out to others (to be able to touch, care, and commit to another person). Sexual intimacy is the first moral mountain that most of us encounter. Thus lifelong sexual contact is a significant moral issue.

I want only to list here some of the ripping characteristics and consequences that follow the splitting out of sexual energy from the adult markers of vocation and marriage. Here are some profound reasons for securing the cultural background before genital contact.[4] I use the term "genital contact" to distinguish it from the notion of technical virginity, that is, "everything but penetration." Philip Phenix of Columbia University said long ago that "heavy petting is morally the equivalent of intercourse." We know today that bonding occurs following any kind of sexual activity.

1. *Premature bonding.* Genital contact based on long-term acquaintance sometimes jumps the gun on marriage and its public endorsement of sustaining, lifelong intimacy. When the homework is done on the first half of the pair bonding steps, we can predict that a relationship which enjoys the slightest degree of privacy will move steadily toward cementing the ultimate sexual bond.

Genital contact clears the way for partners to think in terms of full-time access through marriage. It is not uncommon for fifteen- or seventeen-year-olds to show remarkable maturity. Sometimes there is a change in their behavior, a display of adult independence, and sudden imitated adultlike behavior. When the couple approaches their parents with the news that "We're going to have to get married or 'something' is going to happen," insightful parents will discuss marriage but will not invade the privacy of the forming bond—likely embarrassing the couple in seeking the details of their genital contact. Bonding is powerful and has a remarkably good chance of lifelong survival if the families can surround the bonding couple and protect them.

If the bond is lost or if it is denied for various reasons, the couple becomes vulnerable to depression and, in some cases, suicide. The tragedy of Romeo and Juliet is very much with us today, often hidden in obscure references to sexual frustration in the descriptions of teenage suicide in our news reports. Beyond a shadow of a doubt, the moral integrity of young lovers is at stake. They have encountered an immovable object (the barriers to marriage erected as a protection to teenage moral integrity) with the irresistible force of sexual awareness. Our task is to align the legalities of the marriage process with the sense of intimacy given by God to two people in love.

2. *Desensitizing moral innocence.* Since virtually every-

body is preprogrammed to believe that love happens once forever, the chances for permanence are very slim when sexual intimacy is begun before being securely wrapped in marriage and vocation. Sexual intimacy, once begun, remains forceful throughout any relationship. A couple faces three options if they are unable to marry. (1) Break up and go through extended grief to restore their sense of individual wellness before starting up another relationship. (2) Take the sexual intimacy "underground," thus desensitizing their moral core by leading double lives—as innocent and unmarried, on the one hand, and as sexually intimate, on the other, with deception taking its toll and forfeiting the sharing of the grandest news on earth. (3) Moving in openly to live together, playing house or playing marriage, with the moral desensitizing that comes from violating legal, civil, and moral obligations by which the culture has provided protection for sexual contact, the pair bond, and children.

3. *Deformed sexual appetite.* There is an absolute bonding of sexual pleasure to adult responsibility when a healthy bond develops slowly and is consummated with marriage and first genital contact in close proximity. Sexual pleasure then tends to sustain the couple through the rigors of daily work, bill paying, obligations, and parenthood; stress rarely impairs sexual relationships in such couples, since their bond was forged in the pain of waiting to merge pleasure with full adult responsibility. A tragic bonding pathology often develops when premature genital contact drives the intimacy underground. Premature genital contact tends to separate pleasure from the full adult responsibilities that come with marriage. It is very common for marriages to fail because the premarital "sexual party" was more fun than waking up to financial obligations, parenthood, and the host of adult responsibilities in the real world. It is typical for premaritally intimate couples to be vulnerable to affairs outside the marriage that offer what their early genital contact gave them: pleasure without responsibility—"love them and go home to reality." This schizophrenic "pleasure without work" syndrome is a deadly consequence when it strikes the marriage of the early sexually active couple.

4. *Gateway to promiscuity.* When a bond is lost after long

and patient building, most of our cultures pressure us to start dating again immediately. A person who loses a bond, however, should take time to grieve. This time of mourning is rarely completed within a year, although that is the traditional time expected to grieve for one's loss. When dating begins before the grief process is completed, intimacy tends to begin instantly at the point the more experienced of the two persons reached in a previous relationship. So without healing from the loss and with a repertoire of gratification of touch and perhaps sexual contact, the relationship is in jeopardy. As it breaks, the date-around syndrome resumes and a cycle of one-night stands occurs. Pleasure and responsibility are deliberately split, and a promiscuous lifestyle begins.

5. *Promiscuity and damaged self-esteem.* Perhaps this is the most painful consequence of premature sexual experience. When anyone is used by another person for simple pleasure, self-esteem is extinguished quickly. While there may at first seem to be an attachment, it tends to be out of fear of being abandoned as "trash" for having been used as an object. The line of reasoning, rarely at a conscious level, runs something like this: "I was used. That's what I am: a sex object. Nobody likes anything about me but what they can use in that way."

If sexual arousal and pleasure are introduced to the child as part of the attachment or conspiracy pact, then the child may develop a fascination with genital pleasure as an end in itself. Merely introducing a child to mild pornography or to sexually explicit movies or television is a form of reductionism. This is the form of low self-esteem that is most resistant to change and is the most promiscuous. It tends to be unable to allow significant attachment without taking a long and painful path back to feeling valued for other than sexual reasons.

6. *Trivializing the mystery.* The privacy of sexual feelings and behaviors, instinctive in healthy people, tends to be desensitized by the media blitz, by sexually explicit movies and television, and by the seducers who stand to profit from the consumption of goods and services related to the sex industries. It is little wonder that healthy intimacy in marriage is almost inversely proportional to the number of sex manuals

the participants have read. The mysteries of intimacy, pro-creation, and parenting seem to flourish when there is a safe environment filled with absolute respect for privacy and con-fidentiality, where each of the participants is taken seriously, accepted, and valued for who they are instead of for how they can perform. Honesty, integrity, and privacy are basic foun-dations for healthy adult sexual expression.

Some people try to offer simple labels and short answers to the agonies of adolescence and sexual frustrations and misadventures. At times, I have been asked, "How far can a couple go?" "Is premarital sex a sin?" The trap of sin is wrapped around sexual testing and fears of failure. We who are parents, mentors, and spiritual guides are among the sin-ners because we have trivialized what God has called very good; we have brutalized the moral sensitivity of our young by mocking their integrity in their sense of awakening love.

The agonies of sexual misadventures are so complex that this is simply a label under which so many more forms appear. People who suffer from low self-esteem related to past sexual abuse or "use" and those suffering affective disorders, sexual "addiction," and long-term broken bonding deserve our best support and help. They can find healing in confidential sup-port groups. They deserve to be transformed before they find themselves using or being used again in the deadly and de-structive circuit of promiscuity.

## Potential Tragedies Rooted in Adolescence

It becomes clear that there is no sure path by which to avoid pain during adolescence. I want to affirm that neither the consequences of suffering through abstinence nor the harvest of trouble that comes through adolescent genital con-tact need foreclose the fulfillment of a full and useful life. On the other hand, I must affirm that there are risks of long-term tragedy flowing from either path.

For example, the rigid and lonely male or female may carry immaculate virginity to the grave as a deformed, cynical, re-sentful person. Whether they have retained their technical innocence by choice or merely by inhibition or lack of oppor-tunity, they may carry their bitterness secretly or openly into singleness or into marriage and remain irritable and unresponsive to love. Sexually active teens, however, may slip into promiscuity or may be stuck with an indelible ghost for the remainder of their lives. Those bonded images or the phantoms of having inflicted or having received dehumanizing gestures of abuse or seduction may haunt the inner life across the decades. Here also, the pain, the guilt, and the frustration may hang like a plague over the single person as well as the married.

It might appear that the pain of sexually active teens is as good an option as the pain of abstinence. If both suffer, why not live out early sexual adventures on invitation and impulse? The pain of sexual activity, however, comes with long-term consequences, while the chief pain of abstinence tends to arrive in the present. What is not so easily seen is the fact that consequences extend for a lifetime and beyond, since the social dimensions of sexual activity begin immediately to mushroom: (1) There are the immediate partners who will carry these ghosts of lost love or damaged-object status throughout their lives. (2) There are the partner's families with the inevitable impact made on the young lover's relationship with parents and grandparents, most often in the form of artful deception and dishonesty in formerly trusted relationships. (3) Beyond the present and past generations, there is a high probability of dealing cards to future generations, that is, through conceptions that claim a right to existence and which carry the signals of their premature conception, telegraphing it to the unborn generations. Sexuality carries the stuff of life.

### The Divine Comedy

It is clear that all of us emerge from adolescence wounded by the battleground in some way or another. Tragedies of many sorts can trap us for all our days, and longer. A divine comedy, however, is also ready in the wings if we can accept both our complete histories and God's complete grace until the histories are fully washed by healing and renewal.

I want to establish the thesis that pain comes with adolescence. A final factor becomes the focus question, "What do you say to suffering?"

As a college sophomore I could not fathom how *The Damnation of Faust* which was clearly a tragedy, could be turned into an opera called *Mefistofele* and called a comedy. I had to see the comedy version of the story performed before I understood. Our family sat there at Indiana University in the stadium one summer night in 1968. We watched the seduction of Faust, and we felt the pull of rewards and consequences. We saw damned souls writhing under red lights below the stage in the very hell to which Faust had agreed to go as the consequence of his choice. Then, suddenly, there was another visitor, a presence, with another offer, another sacrifice, and Faust was suddenly lifted off stage and high above the football field in the darkness beyond the stadium stage. Out of total darkness, we saw Faust lifted from the edge of hell and into the sky toward heaven. A local fire truck and snorkel had done the trick before our eyes, but the affective point had been made. Comedy, it turns out, is more than something merely funny; it is something triumphant for good. Comedy denotes deliverance, the foiling of any demonic plan.

Adult maturity lies beyond the painful trough we call adolescence. We must not imagine that it is the suffering itself that produces radical ethical maturity, it is instead the response to the suffering. Aristotle noted in his *Poetics* that tragedy is characterized not by the change in the hero's fortunes from happiness to misery but because of great error on his part. Comedy, on the other hand, differs from tragedy because in comedy the central figure passing through deep trouble emerges as one who is better than people of the present day. Aeschylus, the classical Greek dramatist, caught the idea clearly in his lines from *Agamemnon:* "Zeus, who guided men to think, has laid it down that wisdom comes alone through suffering. . . . Justice so moves that those only learn who suffer."

The pattern by which suffering is the prerequisite to greatness is everywhere visible. In the Bible there are stories of famous personalities like Job, Moses, Jesus, Peter, and Paul, all of whom endured enormous pain and losses, but whose lives were likely thus so charged as to leave a visible mark in history because of the maturity that came through suffering.

So it is with a life full of suffering through doing violence, then repenting of it, and afterward suffering at the hands of others that the Apostle Paul writes: "Our hope for you is firm, because we know that just as you share in our sufferings, so also you share in our comfort" (2 Cor. 1:7).

The ancient wisdom from Ecclesiastes also offers unexpected advice on suffering: "Sorrow is better than laughter, because a sad face is good for the heart. The heart of the wise is in the house of mourning, but the heart of fools is in the house of pleasure" (Eccles. 7:3-4).

For those who know suffering it is not surprising that when God wanted to invade history to make a profound intervention, he sent his Son, Jesus. The unfolding birth, life, death, and resurrection of Jesus is one punctuated by prototypic kinds of pain. He became poor, entered into our human condition with its specific fears, sufferings, shames, and deaths. We hear his commitment to identify with the suffering among us when he opened his public ministry: "'The Spirit of the Lord is on me, because he has anointed me to preach good news to the poor. He has sent me to proclaim freedom for the prisoners and recovery of sight for the blind, to release the oppressed, to proclaim the year of the Lord's favor'" (Luke 4:18-19).

I heard recently of a pastor who called a seventeen-year-old woman to the platform in a Sunday evening service. He announced there with her beside him that she was pregnant out of wedlock, then he demanded that she apologize to the congregation. The Gospel of Matthew draws a picture of Jesus that makes such public humiliation unbelievably pagan. He cites Isaiah's picture of the redeeming servant of God: "'Here is my servant whom I have chosen, the one I love, in whom I delight; I will put my Spirit on him, and he will proclaim justice to the nations. He will not quarrel or cry out; no one will hear his voice in the streets. A bruised reed he will not break, and a smoldering wick he will not snuff out, till he leads justice to victory. In his name the nations will put their hope'" (Matt. 12:18-21).

In this chapter, I have wanted you to wrestle with pain. I am eager to know that you, like me, have some pockets of pain that are still tender out of the years from twelve to twenty-five. I urge you to embrace the pain, to see it as a friend, and to let your own acceptance meet the mystery of grace that can transform pain into maturity—at any age. Most of all, if you are like me, a parent or a grandparent, I want you to take a calm look at your own past adolescence with its turbulence and compare it with what you see in your children's and your grandchildren's experience between fifteen and twenty-five. I want you to see them as full of hope, as candidates for having to deal with the pain of adolescence, and as needing all of the combined resources we can put at their disposal as they pass through on their life voyage. If you can see them in this realistic way, I am confident you can be a more effective guide and friend to them through whatever pain and agony they must bear as they enter into adult responsibility and freedom.

## QUESTIONS PEOPLE ASK

*Q: You make me think God really did make a mistake in fixing it so early pubescence comes to those who have to wait the longest. I had no idea that things have changed so much or that the task of becoming an adult is so different in other cultures. I really feel sorry for my teenagers.*

A: Feeling sorry for them will likely mess everything up. Many parents feel pity and effectively turn their children over to the world, the flesh, and the devil—through instant gratification. What your teens need most is a parent who can say in the same breath, "I know this is a tough time, but it will turn you into a responsible father or mother, and it is worth suffering a little bit now in order to keep your integrity for the rest of your life." A little sympathetic encouragement is a tremendous anchor for a child or a teen. Pity always muddies the water and confuses everybody. Even the parent who stoops to pity, soon gets drawn into self-pity, and tends to drift back into some irresponsibility as if reliving adolescence again.

*Q: What is going to happen to primitive cultures that are quickly jerked into industrial or technological cultures? Isn't that likely to confuse their moral codes and their family life?*

**A:** Precisely. That is why it is critical that we not contaminate a culture by importing our cultural symbols when we have gospel or industrial contact with them. When Christian teachings about grace and God's forgiveness are introduced into a primitive or agrarian culture, we sometimes seem to trivialize issues of reciprocity and restitution and expiation for making wrongs right. This frequently leads to a Gospel of Whoopee! by which the idea is "Do whatever feels good because you can be forgiven by just saying words in a ritual prayer." To a certain extent we see this trivialization of God's character and God's grace in any culture when the full weight of moral responsibility is lifted and mere lip service takes the place of serious responsibilities for moral decisions and behavior. Today's missions—informed by developmental anthropology—find ways of letting God's revelation and grace work within the culture in some amazing and beautiful ways, but we have seen far too many violations of culture by earnest missionary work.

# 6

## Family Losses in a Technological Age

△

I was born in the summer of 1928. Life may not have been easy or our circumstances affluent in western Kansas in those years of crashing stock markets, dust bowls, and infestations of grasshoppers in plague proportions. That life, however, was good, and it was rich in texture, color, and emotion.

By the year I started in Miss Marie's first grade in Fowler, I was old enough to learn almost all of the farming operation. I had been a witness to many of its arenas since my birth, no doubt, but my role was that of spectator. Now I was to be a participant. I cannot remember the day I learned to milk a cow. I suppose that I had been allowed to experiment with pulling the milk down and out of the cow's udder. I had regularly stood close enough to smell the unusual aroma of fresh milk gathering warm and golden in the bucket Daddy held between his legs as he balanced on a one-legged "T" stool. He made a small version of the stool for me, and I had a small bucket. I could feed the cats the milk I could get Daddy to pull into my bucket. It was a game. It was my Daddy's all-day-long game, and it was fun doing what he did.

Life became serious at age six. Now I was awakened

before six o'clock in the morning. "Donnie, I need you to help me milk the cows. Be ready quickly." So I was up. It was our game, and my Daddy and I played the game together.

I have early memories of home, inside the house, beside the wood-burning heating stove in winter, and lying in front of the water-cooled fan during hot summer afternoons after lunch. Most of my early memories were burned into indelible images of my own active participation in the farm operation. The scenes involve the milking barn, the farrowing shed where pigs were born, the chicken houses where I gathered eggs and where kittens often were born. I remember the machine shed with its magical instruments of planting, tilling, cutting, and threshing, and the many acres of fields.

I knew every crevice, every winding cranny where the rain consistently washed ditches through a plowed or planted field. It was my soil. I knew it all and I was learning how to manage everything, how to repair the machines, and how to do man's work. I had no idea that I would ever do anything else. "So this is what 'work' is," I thought. "It's play. It is doing what you love to do all day long and, in some seasons, deep into the darkness, too."

I had to hurry after the early morning milking, because the bus came at 7:30 to take me to school. Miss Marie had things for me to do. They were called assignments and required books. They were fun, too, so I learned to split my day between doing my "pretend you're a Daddy" work on the farm, and my schoolwork for Miss Marie.

I was home by 4:30 in the afternoon. Climbing off the bus, I was eager to get back into my real work clothes that smelled of morning chores. These were comfortable clothes. They had the cut and the fabric of manliness, and they smelled like manly work. I had to do the chores, but it was like playing. If Daddy was away selling a load of hogs or calves, I could go ahead and start the milking.

"Start the milking if you get home before I do," Daddy would say as we finished morning chores. I was only a child, but I could do all the work. Daddy had taught me and had watched me do it. Sometimes I did start the milking before he got home. Occasionally I was completely through with the cream separator game before Daddy got home. I was a man, if only in my Daddy's eyes. I could do the whole thing by myself.

Mother would ask me, "Did you remember to gather the eggs?" Daddy would say, "Did you remember to give Jersey the extra bran while you milked her?" It was unfair, in a way, to give her extra bran, but Jersey gave so much rich milk that Daddy said she earned extra bran and more than paid for it when we sold the cream each week. We kept the cream refrigerated, then twice a week we sent the five-gallon can of pure sweet cream to Beatrice Creamery in Kansas City. The can came back with a check we could use for grocery money.

Of course I knew how to take care of all the daily farm chores. I could do it when I was six or seven. I had been watching and practicing Daddy's work, now, for nearly five years, so how could I be so dumb not to know how to do everything Daddy had to do. He taught me, and he was a good teacher.

I have given you a window into the life of a child of modest opportunity in a rugged and bleak part of the world of 1928 through 1935. I did not leave that daily routine until I turned seventeen, eleven years later. Many times I took full responsibility for major operations for several days at a time while my family was visiting out of state or away on farm business.

I give you this chunk of memory not because it is unique. I give it to you, instead, because there were hundreds of thousands of children who were being reared with those kinds of home experiences. So I offer it because it can be useful here; it contains a slice of human development very much like the billions of slices of children's lives in every culture since the dawn of Creation. Only the particulars of "Daddy's work" and "Mother's work" would be different across cultures and centuries. The ways of learning and becoming a mature person have remained the same—until now. Therein lies the urgency of this book. Things are different. Values and traditions are in transition. It is critical that we who have any word of hope stretch ourselves across the canyon as a bridge to solid, universal, and unchanging realities in the new and coming generation.

From the dawn of history until World War II, parents

taught their children everything they knew about their work. Children learned the basics during the years when they regarded work as play. Parents would craft tiny specimen models of adult tools and smile as they watched the children imitate adult work and call it play.

Now, half a century and more later, children operate electronic toys with joy sticks and remote controls. Virtually nothing they play with as children resembles their parents' tools. The toy models are not scaled down tools of trade and work but of recreation and adult play: all-terrain-vehicles, sports cars, 4 × 4s, transformers, motor bikes, and war games.

What has happened? It would be easy to say that we are more affluent now and have moved to the cities and away from the soil. That may be true, but it likely does not explain what happened to the magic years of children learning about adult work.

We could point out that progress has brought us more and finer equipment to deliver us from menial tasks like milking cows. We are no longer preoccupied with work but rather leisure and play. That too is true. Indeed we have virtually wiped out what rural families used to call chores. There are no more under-the-bed commodes to empty each morning. Many families do not wash, dry, and store dishes three times a day. Farming is mechanized and motorized, and much farm equipment is air-conditioned. Farms boast of one-man operation equipment for crop management tasks. Around the house high speed vacuum cleaners make an hour's work of what once took two or three people most of a day.

## The Double Fault

It would have been one thing to postpone vocation and marriage for our adolescents if we could have given them an authentic sense of being needed, of making a significant contribution to the household as a means of harnessing some of that sexual energy of the postponement years. Instead, we have closed down the shop of labor for children and teens. We have taken away their childhood play-at-work apprenticeships in the company of significant adults. They have become the generation of the bored.

By our lack of imagination we have defaulted, and our young now tend to expect that the years from thirteen to marriage are a free ticket, and that parents should pick up the tab for their entertainment. We have double faulted. Perhaps it is a triple fault. We have at the very same time created a society in which sexual maturity arrives earlier, but we have also postponed their entry into adult responsibility. We have created a culture of entertainment, leisure, and play to replace primary parental teaching through the luxury of parent-child partnership at meaningful work.

Perhaps no one has diagnosed the ills of the American family better than Urie Bronfenbrenner of Cornell University.

America's families, and their children, are in trouble, so deep and pervasive as to threaten the future of our nation. The source of the trouble is nothing less than a national neglect of children and those primarily engaged in their care—America's parents.

We like to think of America as a child-centered society, but our actions belie our words. A hard look at our institutions and way of life reveals that our national priorities lie elsewhere. The pursuit of affluence, the worship of material things, the hard sell and the soft, the willingness to accept technology as a substitute for human relationships, the imposition of responsibility without support, and the readiness to blame the victims of evil for the evil itself have brought us to the point where a broken television set or a broken computer provokes more indignation and more action than a broken family or a broken child.

Our national rhetoric notwithstanding, the actual patterns of life in America today are such that children and families come last. Our society expects its citizens first of all to meet the demands of their jobs and then to fulfill civic and social obligations. Responsibilities to children are to be met, of course, but this is something one is expected to do in spare time. . . .

The frustrations are greatest for the family of poverty where the capacity for human response is crippled by hunger, cold, filth, sickness, and despair. No parent who spends days in search of menial work and nights in keeping rats away from the crib can be expected to find the time—let alone the heart—to engage in constructive activities with children or to serve as a stable source of love and discipline.

For families who can get along, the rats are gone, but the rat race remains. The demands of a job, or often two jobs, that claim mealtimes, evenings, and weekends as well as days, the trips and moves one must make to get ahead or simply hold one's own, the ever-increasing time spent in commuting, the parties, evenings out, social and community obligations—all things one has to do if one is to meet primary responsibilities—produce a situation in which a child often spends more time with a passive babysitter than with a participating parent.

And even when the parent is at home, a compelling force cuts off communication and response among the family members. And though television could, if used creatively, enrich the activities of children and families, it now only undermines them. Like the sorcerer of old, the television set casts its magic spell, freezing speech and action, and turning the living into silent statues so long as the enchantment lasts. The primary danger of the television screen lies not so much in the behavior it produces as in the behavior it prevents—the talks, the games, the family festivities and arguments through which much of the child's learning takes place and the character is formed. Turning on the television set can turn off the process that transforms children into people.

In our modern way of life, it is not only parents of whom children are deprived, it is people in general. A host of factors conspires to isolate children from the rest of society. The fragmentation of the extended family, the separation of residential and business areas, the disappearance of neighborhoods, zoning ordinances, occupational mobility, child labor laws, the abolishment of the apprentice system, consolidated schools, television, separate patterns of social life for different age groups, the working mother, the delegation of child care to specialists—all these manifestations of progress operate to decrease opportunity and incentive for meaningful contact between children and persons older or younger than themselves.

And here we confront a fundamental and disturbing fact: *children need adults in order to become human*. The fact is fundamental because it is firmly grounded both in scientific research and in human experience. It is disturbing because the isolation of children from adults simultaneously threatens the growth of the individual and the survival of the society. The young cannot pull themselves up by their own bootstraps. It is primarily through observing, playing, and working with others older and younger than themselves that children discover both what they can do and who they can become, that they develop both their ability and their identity. It is primarily through exposure and interaction with adults and children of different ages that a child acquires new interests and skills, and learns the meaning of tolerance, cooperation, and compassion. Hence to relegate children to a world of their own is to deprive them of their humanity and ourselves as well.

Yet this is what is happening in America today. *We are experiencing a breakdown in the process of making human beings human. The failure to reorder our priorities, the insistence on business as usual, and the continual reliance on rhetoric as a substitute for fundamental reforms can only have one result: the far more rapid and pervasive growth of alienation, apathy, drugs, delinquency, and violence among the young, and not so young, in all segments of our national life. We face the prospect of a society which resents its own children and fears its youth.* Surely this is a road to national destruction. . . . What is needed is a change in our patterns of living which will once again *bring people back into the lives of children and children back into the lives of adults.*[1]

## Rich Kids in a Sterile World

If we have taken meaningful work and significant family relationships away from children by our preoccupation with our own social and economic pursuits, we should not be surprised to find that the children get the messages: "You're on your own, kid!" and "Hang on to your peers!"

Where do they turn? Many of them turn to the playthings adults provide: television, entertainment, motor vehicles, and music. Most of these pacifiers are passive substitutes for real relationships and meaningful experience in adult work. For the more socially motivated among them, they turn to their agemates for social contact, but their peers tend to be as impoverished and confused as they are. They don't have much to give each other. Yet we continue to herd them together into schools organized to bring more and more children together who are more and more alike as to age, grade, and ability. The result is a new and massed conglomerate of coldness, anonymity, and often violence. Add to this the fact that their lives are increasingly sterile of significant experience and relationships with people older and younger with whom they share some community life outside their work-place, the school.

On the out-of-school front, they tend to satiate themselves with endless hours of music videos and who knows what on cable television. All these diversions tend to be furnished by guilt-ridden parents who feel a need to atone for making their children latchkey kids. Because they live in isolation from the adults they need the most, this lifestyle becomes intolerable or boring, and the young turn inward.

Loneliness is the deepening chasm that plagues our young. Study any set of statistics on depression, eating disorders, and suicide, and we get a picture that our present way of dealing with children is coming at a very high price.

Who can say exactly how our present crisis of values has developed? We can describe the loss of significant parent-child time, the loss of significant parent-child work, and the loss of adults out of the households across the last fifty years. Some researchers using implanted microphones in infant clothing, for example, found father's specific verbal interaction totaling thirty-eight seconds per day.[2] Yet as recently as the late 1940s, one family in ten had an adult relative besides the two parents living under the same roof, thus enriching adult-child contact with joint projects and meaningful exchanges both in words and in work. Today, the new phenomenon is the single-parent family. The third adult, usually a grandparent or single aunt or uncle, has all but disappeared, according to recent census findings. Impoverishment, loss of significant interaction with an adult who has time to listen, is the new order of the family.

Many people conclude that children are only one layer of the victims of the rise of severe individualism. The driving focus becomes "doing what I want when I want to do it." Ironically, the parents who are driven by their own personal ambition create and shape children who will show them how to pursue selfish ambition and to do it with a vengeance, damaging the parents in the process. An amazing piece appeared in *The New Yorker* that at least described some of the effects of this new narcissism:

> If one examines these points of disintegration separately, one finds they have a common cause—the overriding value placed

on the idea of individual emancipation and fulfillment, in the light of which more and more, the old bonds are seen not as enriching but as confining.

We are coming to look upon life as a lone adventure, a great personal odyssey, and there is much in this view which is exhilarating and strengthening. But we seem to be carrying it to such an extreme that if each of us is an Odysseus, he is an Odysseus with no Telemachus to pursue him, with no Ithaca to long for, with no Penelope to return to—an Odysseus on a journey that has been rendered pointless by becoming limitless.

The other side—that we give form and meaning to those solitary destinies through our association with others—has been allowed to fade away, leaving us exposed to a new kind of cold.[3]

It would be one thing if we found ourselves at the mercy of some new killer plague. It is quite another to stand, as many of us do, straddling the generations from the 1930s to the present. It is clear to everyone that the process by which responsible and healthy humans are formed has broken down. There remains an aging generation who can still tell the stories about times when children had an important place in the lives of adults and when children found adults eager to promote them to adult ranks and responsibilities and rewards at early ages. We cannot hide from the fact that we seem to have learned how to destroy our children and we tend to be sticking our heads in the sand refusing to examine our new ways of launching families that are failing us all so miserably.

## Transforming Priorities and Values

We confront the most critical question yet. Given the technological culture and our preoccupation with success and affluence, we may find that we cannot take even the first step toward recovering intimate adult-child comradeship in our culture.

On the other hand, many of us are ready to try. In this book I am putting down the best strategies I know to bring vital connections back into families. Fortunately we have very impressive research models that we can confidently report are working to launch effective and strong families in this technological age.

To begin, can we list the values we need to bring back to our homes and our culture?

1. Time in which children are brought significantly into the lives of adults and adults are brought back into the lives of children.
2. Meaningful work/play experiences that are productive tutorials of later adult vocations, rehearsals for adult responsibilities.
3. Spontaneous exchange of stories, questions, and tales of happiness and pain between adults and children.

Could we list priorities? Can we say what we really want and in what order the list is arranged? Here is a beginning list:

1. What would my day look like if time with children were a top priority instead of canceling the children's time first if there is a social or an economic reason for doing so?
2. What part of the household operation might be distributed to include parent-child teamwork to handle routine, even drudgery jobs?
3. How could I bring my children into my vocational experience, given laws about safety and school attendance, and given my need to conform to adults-only expectations and protocol where I work?
4. How might children and adults be brought together instead of segregated in virtually all aspects of community, school, and church life?
5. How can I bring relatives, grandparents, even surrogate relatives into significant work, recreation, and learning time with my children? Are there populations of older people concentrated in institutional settings who might be available for contact with children from churches or schools? Are there older people available near a children's day-care center? Are they operated side-by-side to enhance probable contact and intentional programs bringing the old and the young together in the care facility?

If Urie Bronfenbrenner can paint a bleak picture of what is, perhaps we can begin to sketch what might be in a brighter scenario. It is clear that trends can be changed so long as we are willing to try to contemplate what is happening.

In this chapter, I have wanted you to wrestle with some of the trends and symptoms of a disintegrating family and culture. You are joining me, I am sure, in voting to transform our values and priorities and to find the time to act on those values to put ourselves back into the lives of our children and to bring them back into our lives.

We can predict that if we fail to reorder those priorities and schedules then there is a natural default system that will come up with some holocaust. Not long ago I lost most of a chapter on my computer. The only warning I had was when I hit the "Save and End Edit" key, the system blinked a single warning to the screen—"Fatal Error"—and I was out of the working file, out of the word processing package, and had defaulted all the way back to the operating system. The machine was still humming, but the work was lost.

In the case of a fatal error, the work has to start over, whether on the computer or in Sodom or Pompeii or Los Angeles. We are already getting early signals that things are not predicting well for the future of the human race. Surely we can find a way to surround our children with the health that buys the future for them and for ourselves as well.

### QUESTIONS PEOPLE ASK

*Q: We have done the chores thing around our house for several years, even with lists of distributed responsibilities on the refrigerator door. Frankly, it would take me less time to do most of the things than it does to harp at the children to get them done. I'm not impressed with the chores idea at all.*

A: Me too. Especially since most suburban chores consist of dividing the drudgery and consigning the kids to solitary confinement to slave through the stuff. Can you see that this is exactly the opposite of what I described in this chapter? Chores used to be things parents did with their children. There was rarely the condemnation to having to do them alone. Only an emergency placed solitary pressure on the kid, and that was known to be a test of adult potential and competence. It ought to be a rule of thumb that (1) all household drudgery is co-assigned to one adult and one child, and that (2) no meaningless drudgery is assigned just to torment children with obviously invented busy work. I consider cleaning your own room to be punishment since the whole house needs to be cleaned. Any team effort might easily include the individual rooms, with abundant conversation fueling the three- or four-hour drudgery turning it into one of the nicest visits of the week.

*Q: We have sent our children to my father's farm in another state since they were pre-teens. Now that they are in high school, they really count on going there. They even hire out to my Dad's neighbors there for light farm jobs and earn a little money, but something is different when they come home. I have a hard time getting them to do anything around here at all, yet my parents comment on how responsible they are in the country. What is going on?*

**A:** It is hard to speculate on all of the possible dimensions of the scenario you describe, but we know that suburbia is a very boring place to grow up. The look-alike houses all in a row may be neat and attractive, but the sameness of a freeway or a subdivision tends to turn us all a little numb. Our children's boredom, their vulnerability to plastic entertainment, and their occasional tendencies toward violence may in fact be related to the plastic appearance of their suburban environment. Humans not only need space—we are territorial creatures in some profound way—we also need diversity. We need unknown space to explore, unpredictable paths to walk, living space unique to ourselves. From time immemorial, cities have been centers of intense social problems. Yet look where we are all headed today—packing ourselves like panicked rats into a pile in a most unhealthy pattern of living.

# 7

# *Risk Proofing Your Kids*

△

I picked up Jason, whisking him off with me to do a university retreat at Wesley Woods, an hour east of Lexington. The Wesley Foundation students from Morehead State University had planned the event, and I had been to the site a couple of times earlier.

Jason was then about nine years old, and I had spotted a fishing pond at Wesley Woods that was alive with bream. I remembered that fishing gear was furnished at the resort. I was not ready for the conversation that emerged as soon as Jason was in the car.

"Grandpa," he began, "I feel really lucky. At Pepperhill Farm where I go every day, I'm practically the only kid who has a real family. I am really lucky. I have a Daddy, a Mother, a brother, and a sister. I haven't found anybody else that has a whole family."

"What do they have?" I probed, knowing that his mother, a social worker, was beating the bushes in Lexington to locate children in disadvantaged circumstances who were eligible for the day camp at Pepperhill Farm just fifteen minutes from downtown. I knew, too, that Jason's wonderful summer of swimming and living in the sun at Pepperhill was one of his mother's perks.

"Not much, and when I hear that they don't have a Daddy or even a Mother, I wonder how they get along. Some of them just live with relatives.

"I feel really lucky, too, because at our house any of us can say exactly how we feel. Most of the kids say they don't dare tell anybody how they feel. They say they'll get slapped or hurt if they do, but at our house everybody listens to how we feel."

In our search for effective ways to launch integrity children in an age of promiscuity, one important piece of the evidence turns up here. We now know the characteristics of children who are least at risk to the seduction of alcohol, drugs, and sex.

I have boiled down some of the clearest findings. So here I will describe five of those characteristics. They deal with role identity, a sense of competency, a feeling of connectedness, the grasp of leverage, and (not surprisingly) self-discipline,[1] but let me first turn on the flashing lights that warn of dangerous ways families sometimes put their children at risk.

### Caution: Kids at Risk Here

At the most obvious level, let me remind you that children imitate the most admired people on earth—their parents. This means that no amount of instruction, threat, or payoff is likely to keep them from following in your tracks.

Parents who are compulsive in any emotional or behavior pattern should not be surprised to see their compulsion duplicated in their children by the midteen years. Often the imitation is visible in the preschool years. Let me name a few: compulsive eating, violent temper, alcohol, narcotics, multiple sex partners. In a few cases the children imitate because it seems like a good thing to do—an admired behavior is being rehearsed and incorporated into the child's adult aspirations. More often, however, the child will detest the parent's promiscuity, drug abuse, alcoholism, eating disorders, or rage. Indeed, these children often declare that they will never do the awful things you do. In the crunch of the increasing responsibilities of adolescence and adulthood, however, the compulsive option becomes a way to cope. The strategy has been tutored by an unwitting but effective teacher—parent values and behavior. For this reason, swinging, sexually active single parents are actually instructing their children in promiscuity. There is every reason for parents to enter compulsion therapy, engage a support group for accountability, and form a healthy personal integrity as a first step in launching healthy children into adolescence and adulthood.

At a much deeper level, a troubled marriage or an anxious parent may telegraph to a child a sense of ambiguity, uncertainty, even a signal that triggers fear of the collapse of the family in its present form. With divorce shattering so many children's worlds, an unresolved parental quarrel, a stone-walled silence that puts up barriers between parents, or dumping marital unhappiness everywhere is sure to unsettle the children. Even when no words or violence go on record, the emotions are read infallibly. The interruption of gestures of affection between parents, the extended hours separated by work—such simple things do not fool children. They have an uncanny ability to infer when a change in family patterns is a signal of trouble in the family.

I have worked closely with families after the death of a parent. Even in cases where family solidarity seems to increase as members close ranks to protect each other, the loss of a parent seems to damage some internal gyroscope governing sexual integrity. Young men particularly seem to be at risk following the death of either parent. They often fall quickly into the arms of a woman. The collapse of sexual integrity seems unrelated to the ripeness of the young lovers' relationship, but rather mysteriously linked to the disappearance of an affectional harbor on which the boy depended. I have speculated that grief itself makes us all vulnerable in our affective center—our emotions, in which our sexual responses have been developed. Yet it may also be that young males, in some literal way, need to move from father and mother and to cleave to a wife, in the exact formula of Eden.

We are going to look now at the internal development of the sense of identity and integrity as the major core on which we can do constructive parenting as we work to risk proof our kids against alcohol, sex, and drugs. In chapters 8, 9, 10, and

11, we will return to look at family systems. It is, after all, in the structure and health of the marriage-family-parent-child network itself that the child is most protected or put at risk.

## Role Identity

One of those built-in magnets God plants in humans is the yearning to find a model on which to gaze while learning through imitation. However much we may fear the dangers of inappropriate imitation, the fact is that becoming human is profoundly based on such imitation.

Children learn their vocabularies and patterns of speech almost entirely through imitation. All of us learned to walk, how to carry our bodies, and a whole arsenal of gestures through imitation. At the core of this imitation is what we call "role identity." By this we refer to the intentional copying of sex-appropriate behavior of a respected mature person of the same gender. Within role identity fall all of those gestures, behaviors, and ways of relating to the opposite sex that have anything to do with what we call masculinity or femininity. Elsewhere I note the specific deficits that are predictable in father-absent situations and speculate about likely effects of the loss of a mother.[2]

If we care about growing healthy adults out of our own and other people's children, we simply must guarantee that their early years are populated with significant role models. The mother and father relationships are, of course, the ones custom fitted for this task. The first building block in risk proofing a child against adolescent temptations is painfully missing if a parent is either not consistently available or does not delight in the potential hours of exchange with the child in routine and special parenting tasks.

David reported to me that his father had no time for him, but he was lucky to have a neighbor with a son about David's own age. From the earliest years, David picked up on the available model next door, and to this day is stabilized by the next-door fathering he got. His story emerged when I began to work with about fifty men using some of the agenda coming out of Peter Druck's work with men. He found that many men have unfinished business with their fathers.[3] That agenda,

Druck found, often leaves men emotionally frozen. David turned himself in privately to open the subject. He was dealing with long-term resentment against his natural father because he took no time to be with him, his only method of trying to shape him was by criticizing him.

Interference with mothering leaves devastating effects, as well. Most often the stories of mother deprivation involve her death or her addiction to alcohol or drugs.

While you can hear the signals of the child of five or older, the impressions imprinted on the younger child are evidently even stronger. These preverbalized imprints cast a long shadow on the child's acquisition of language, body carriage, and mannerisms.

My son, Mike, at age three was spending the afternoon with me in my office. My staff joined me there for fifteen minutes in midafternoon. Mike was a longstanding favorite of theirs so, of course, he had his juice and cookie right along with us. In that setting, I had a habit of enjoying the full outdoorscape of the lovely pond and rolling lawn that runs between office complexes there at Winona Lake. I would desecrate the marble window sill by planting my right foot on the sill and slouching to drink my coffee and visit. At one point the staff was obviously amused with something, repeatedly glancing first at me and then behind me. I wondered what private joke these people were enjoying at my expense. Turning to look behind me, I saw a wonderful thing. There stood my Mickey with his right foot firmly planted on top of the heating unit that ran at just the right height to allow him to imitate my posture perfectly while standing only inches behind me and out of my sight.

Our sons and their wives are much more aware of the importance of parent-child identity than we were. When Justin was four, we took him with Lesli, his six-year-old sister, for two weeks while I was in Chicago and on to a week of family camp at Sky Lodge in Wisconsin. Before we left, Mike got my full attention and then explained fairly intently, "Now I want you to put at least five minutes each evening into roughhousing with Justin—on the floor or on the bed. He needs to be wrestled with at least that much every day."

You can recount your own observations. What I want you

to be aware of is that this curriculum is rolling during all of the child's waking hours. So when the parent is indifferent, or is on the road, or otherwise unable or unwilling to allow extended time with the child, we may predict that role identity may be deficient. During the preschool years, it may become urgent for both father and mother to look at their job situations and to protect daily contact time, curbing social uses of evenings, and turning up the volume on high interactive daily episodes of play, reading, and conversation with the young children. The choice of day care or sitter services needs to be made, too, on the basis of role-imitation value of the care-givers.

When the mother and father are not available for any reason, it becomes critical for the single parent or the guardian to look carefully at the other role models who might be surrogate-substitutes for the missing or dysfunctional parent. The best surrogates tend to be grandparents, uncles, aunts, or neighbors. If the child accumulates more than three hours per week in the care of a teacher, youth minister, or coach, you are likely to see the magnet strike up the magic role imitation if the child is aged five or older.

Indeed, with healthy and available parents, we see the support of surrogate models show up in the table conversations. "Mr. Hooper says . . ."; "Mr. Hooper doesn't do it that way"; " Mr. Hooper does it this way." You will smile and wonder why this Mr. Hooper suddenly became such a powerful influence in your child's life, and you may pray that he is worth imitating. As a child moves toward pubescence, this magnet seeks outside models as if to prepare the child to leave the nest. So it becomes critical to the parents to place the child in environments in which the most worthy models are abundant. This is one major reason why the school, church, recreation, and club environments are worth looking at carefully.

Once launched into the school years, the role identification task is both more complicated and less focused on the parents. Now the child is both exposed to more models and is able to discriminate among many models and to describe the admired persons. Parent-child time, during all of childhood and launching, deserves to revolve around predictable episodes of focused conversation on positive and enjoyable topics. Correction and discipline are, of course, major responsibilities of the parents, but most of us carry that load without prompting. What we tend to miss more often are the intentional blocks of time at the table or before bedtime in which we focus on the child by reviewing the day's events, by affirming the child's qualities, and by anticipating the coming good things that tomorrow and the weeks ahead bring. Prayer with a child at bedtime is perhaps the single most powerful positive review and forecasting time available to any of us.

### A Sense of Competency

"I can do it myself!" are words every parent loves to hear. It is hard to remember that the role-stable child is playing at being the adult of the same sex as the admired parent.

By "competency" the research reporters mean to describe the literal ability of the growing child to accomplish a given task. This is done at a level of performance that both the child and the adults in the environment affirm is done well.

Recall from your memory or consider what you have seen in the last few hours and notice how simply and how confidently a child announces competence by such simple performances:

1. Closing a door.
2. Flushing the toilet.
3. Feeding him or herself.
4. Bringing the mail.
5. Reading the Bible for family prayers.
6. Feeding the pet.
7. Operating the sweeper.
8. Running an errand.
9. Furnishing the taxi service.

The list looks ridiculous. Any of the performances may at last become merely an assignment or chore, but in the beginning, and perhaps for the rest of their lives, they could remain hooked into the pleasure of feeling competent. What we miss so consistently is that the child literally experiences a sense of chemical exhilaration upon each small accomplishment. The love of work is no doubt rooted in those early experiences of the child in which a strong dose of magical pleasure accompanied the first task completion and tended to remedicate with pleasure at each later repetition.

Children with poor work habits when they arrive at school, for example, are consistently children who have not had work laminated to pleasure by doing it with or for an admired adult. Adults who love their work but are not workaholics are frequently heard to say, "I'm sometimes embarrassed to take such a handsome salary for work that I would pay for the privilege of doing here." Consistently, these are people who were nurtured on competency teaching by their parents and who are energized by the thrill of being productive.

When reading the literature on competency I found a deep memory triggered. From my earliest toddlerhood, I was the constant companion of my Dad in those rounds of his farm work that were not deadly dangerous or simply tedious. I got in on the trips to the grain elevator, for example, in the wheat trucks or alfalfa seed runs. Alfalfa seed threshing came late in the season, long after school had begun, so my memories are deep in the preschool years.

I have vivid memories of standing with Dad in the bed of a half-ton 1935 International pickup truck. He was operating the grain augur that was pumping golden alfalfa seed into Beamis bags which stood to about three feet in height when filled with the heavy and valuable seeds. He treated the alfalfa seed as if it were literally gold. I can recall that the sacks were almost as tall as I was at the time, but with each shutdown of the flow of seed, Daddy would quickly gather the cloth to tie the bag, wrap a single strand of twine around the gathered top, cinch it up tight, then say to me, "Donnie, I need your finger."

Today I can still feel a slight memory of sensation in that left index finger. I would place it over the "X" formed by the first effort at a miller's knot in the twine and would press hard. Then Dad would make another knot and pull it down against my tiny finger. When it was touching my finger, Dad would say, "Now pull your finger out." I would slip it out and he would whack the miller's knot down to make an almost airtight bag of that finely woven Beamis bag. Alfalfa seed was so tiny it would run out anywhere there was the slightest hole.

My memory includes images and sensations of Daddy lifting me over the sideboards of that pickup truck, standing me on a running board and telling me to jump inside on the driver's seat. As I sat there or even stood to see out the windshield, Daddy would slap my leg or punch my shoulder and affirm me: "Donnie, you were a big help to me. I would never have been able to tie those sacks without you."

At some level, I knew he was right. Anybody could see you needed somebody's finger to hold the first hitch in the knot while you gathered the second one.

We would take the seed to town to sell it. It was a two-and-a-half-mile ride. We were men together on those drives to sell the seed. One day we stopped by a Chevrolet dealer to look at the new cars on the showroom floor. This was an important and manly thing to be doing, especially since we had never had a new car in all of my life (and would not have one until fifteen years later when it became our wedding gift). I remember asking Daddy how much the new Chevy cost. I can still see it, a 1932, black four-door. "The car costs exactly the same amount of money as the check we just got from the exchange for that load of alfalfa seed," my Daddy said.

So I was beginning to see how work produces alfalfa seed, which turns into money, which might be traded for a new car. Money was how you changed your work into things you needed to buy.

A sense of competency, of being able to execute even the smallest task well enough to evoke recognition—that is one of the foundations a child can lay down to reduce later risk to vulnerability to drugs, alcohol, and inappropriate sexual activities.

### A Feeling of Connectedness

Here we confront a deep need of every human being, but one that is seriously threatened today. By "connectedness" we refer to the awareness that there are other people of importance in the family chain of generations and relationships.

Here are links to the past, to the future, and laterally to the people who share the same roots and the same values.

At a wider level, connectedness refers to the sense that the generations of a given community have importance to each other, that there is a common glue that holds the social fabric together.

When you ask how this sense of connectedness might be formed, it becomes clear again that significant contact is the key. In chapter 6 we looked at the breakdown in all of the connections of society—the breaking out of the nuclear family from its tribal network and the layering of society such that people tend to be connected only to people of the same age and job. It is clear that this risk proofing component is under serious threat.

It is, however, not entirely beyond our reach. David and Helen Seamands tell how their son Steve grew up both in India where they were missionaries and in the United States where they furloughed and eventually settled in pastoral ministry. After he was married and the father of their grandchildren, Steve reported that very often when he was a teenager and was tempted to run with the fast lane crowd in some compromising activity he would remember a photograph of his infant baptism in India. His grandfather, "Tata" Seamands, was holding him in the baptismal service. That picture was firmly imprinted in Steve's mind. He could not forget it. The image of Tata and the family connection evoked a sense of destiny that never left him.

"I would think of that picture—my godly grandfather holding me in his arms—and I would say to myself, 'This is who I am. I am a part of a covenant family. How can I ever turn away from that?'"

The sense of connectedness is more than the warm feelings we have when we are together. Our connection to our roots links us to the important models and to our idea of what their values were or are.

A similar sense of connectedness links us to our future. It is not so easily and vividly put in images, of course, but children have a sense that someday they will be parents.

I was impressed by that logic of the future connections several years ago when I read Kenneth and Alice Hamilton's bold reasoning in *To Be a Man—To Be a Woman:* "Often it is argued that an individual's sexual conduct is his [or her] own business, so long as no one else is being hurt. Yet sexuality is never just a matter between two individuals, because in every sexual act procreation is made either possible or impossible. The next generation is involved."[4]

Not only in sexual behavior, but in all moral and social behavior, the future generations gather as a cloud of unborn witnesses as if to say: "Go slow. Choose well. You are setting the agenda for us. If you indulge, our health, our emotional stability, and our vulnerability to addictions or dependencies is in your hands." None of us lives to ourselves or chooses only for ourselves. We are always connected.

This feeling of connectedness is likely most nurtured by keeping significant celebrations, by focusing birthday and anniversary conversations to roots and to the future. The past is easy to bring into present connection by recalling funny or otherwise wonderful stories, by using photographs or movies, and by occasional positive reference to relatives' hopes for today's child or teen. The future is also easy to bring into the present as we speculate about it—how many years it will be until sitting in this very room we expect to welcome a son or daughter-in-law and grandchildren. I frequently say to my grandchildren, "I hope you live to see your children's children. It is so much fun knowing you and watching you grow up, that I want it to happen again for you." This imagination is a connection with an unspecific future, and planted in early and middle childhood it never infringes inappropriately on their sense of privacy or freedom to choose for themselves.

The feeling of community connectedness is virtually impossible to generate unless your family is heavily involved in intergenerational, multicultural organizations. The schools have entirely failed us today in this domain. They are grouping children and teens who increasingly are more and more alike. Teachers tend to be unknown to the family members. Bus drivers are anonymous strangers from somewhere else in the metroplex. Custodians are contracted technocrats. During my childhood these people were significant community members, known to my parents, and regular in church attendance at places where I saw them. Today it becomes critical that intergenerational contacts be made through churches, vocational organizations, and service affiliations if our children are to know enough about persons older or younger than themselves to feel a sense of identity through attachment to them.

## A Grasp of Leverage

By leverage I mean the power people have over their own future. There is lateral leverage, of course, by which a person has a sense of being able to make a difference through the expressing of a judgment or a preference. Voting is exercising this sort of lateral leverage, and children and teens rarely have this privilege.

The really important sense of power is over one's own life and destiny. Children least at risk to popular seductions are those who feel that they can make decisions today which will make visible differences tomorrow. Vast numbers of our young feel impotent—unable to shape, make, or influence the future. The cry of youth in a nuclear age is "There is no tomorrow. Grab all the gusto you can while you can." The older version, the Epicurean motto, was simply "Eat, drink, and be merry, for tomorrow we die." Fire-and-brimstone evangelists from my childhood left Garrison Keillor and me hoping secretly that Jesus would not come back in the final judgment and end the world until we had got married and had sex, at least once. I doubt there are many children and teens today who fear the eschatological end of the world, but their generation has every reason to shudder lest a nuclear winter steal their adult opportunities from them. "Tomorrow we die," therefore, must be at some profound and interior level the great seducer.

Most modern Epicureans eat, drink, and party so as not to contemplate the empty future. Their goal is to so anesthetize themselves into numbness that they will forget how bleak the future appears to be. Now many of them would deny this dim view of their own future, but the frustration and anxiety would emerge if you could ever bring them down from their artificial world of faking a party long enough to do any serious reflecting and talking. Indeed, we are now deep enough into several generations of escapism as a way of life that our children imitate our party life as if it were the adult vocation. Their favorite toys are less often miniatures of adult productivity than of adult indulgence. The ATV craze has bonded fathers and sons, for example, to the recreational end of their lives instead of to the productive interests focused on the fathers' work. This trivialization of time may have created an environment in which we actually are teaching our children to be Epicureans.

If so, we have created consumers who imagine that life is one spending spree. The use of credit cards, go-now-pay-later schemes, and patterns of extravagant consumption can set up a deadly prediction for young marriages. Their income levels rarely provide the financial base from which to operate with all of the comforts and gadgets to which they have become accustomed. If their parental bonding has been primarily in the recreation arena, they will find work less than rewarding and recreation highly exhilarating, and wonder how to bring these two contradictory aspects of life together.

Children learn the grasp of leverage from their earliest experiences when cause-and-effect relationships appear. Elsewhere I suggest that children's use of money should begin with the first awareness that "goods and money" are connected.[5] I caution against giving children money in the store or in any environment where they can spend it immediately. They need to have control over the money for several days while they contemplate the things money might do for them. They are luckier still if they discover competing claims for their money, competing desires among which they must make a choice. The best of all worlds arrives when the child needs more money which requires saving today to control tomorrow's arrival of the longed-for object. Mail-order catalogs are especially useful in strengthening this sense of making decisions today that bring delivery at a future date. The daily run to check the mail does wonders for creating and strengthening this sense of leverage on the future.

For children who exist day-by-day, the grasp of leverage on their own futures is most difficult. In households where meals together are rare and where one's personal property is not respected, it becomes important to grab the gusto when it is there. Food in the refrigerator is to eat now. Candy or fruit on the counter is for instant consumption.

"Look at me," Roy announced to his brothers and sisters and parents. "This apple is mine." He then proceeded to lick around the entire delicious apple and placed it in the refrigerator. His "contamination" was the only security for what any of them might take for a stray apple to be consumed on the spot.

Families that keep an open supply of fruit or after-dinner mints are likely displaying one signal that their home is doing well on the leverage issue. The children are not being programmed for instant consumption as a means of survival. The addictive personality tends to have suffered some deprivation and to have seen instant gratification as the essential way of life.

It is easy to see that the grasp of leverage comes by experience. Whenever we can delay the instant gratification of desire and postpone it ever so slightly, we likely are stretching the child's moral courage by allowing repeated surges of anticipation to enhance the strong desire. Ironically, this sort of stretching is easily within the grasp of the affluent family, but it is there that instant gratification, overabundance of gadgets and toys, and easy money tend to blunt if not destroy one of the gifts of moral strength: the development of the appetite to buy the future by waiting today.

### Self-Discipline

Self-discipline shows up in the research lists along with the other characteristics of children least at risk to drugs, alcohol, or premature sexual intimacy. There is, however, a sense in which it is likely a product of the previous four developmental disciplines. By self-discipline we mean, of course, that the individual has developed internal control such that choices of behavior in the world apart from the family are consistent with the choices made in the presence of the family. At the lowest level, self-discipline is sometimes confused with internalization of the parent, in which it seems to have elements of coercion or control involved. At its best, self-discipline tilts toward integrity and suggests high consistency of personhood across changing environments.

"I feel like my days of parenting are almost over," one father said to me, talking of his seventeen-year-old son who was off for a week of skiing with his girlfriend's family. "It worries his mother a great deal to have him in such a stressed moral environment this week, but I have to trust him. We've had seventeen years with him, and I think he can handle the week very well. He knows who he is."

Some things never change. I have a letter in my files from more than twenty years ago. Keith had been in our Sunday school class when we spent about six hours a week with wall-to-wall teens in a great church. Then he was off to the Navy to do his duty. Robbie and I would get occasional letters typed on the Signal Corps keyboard on board ship, with all of the peculiar slashes through numbers. In one of the letters, he described how depressing it was to arrive again at Subic Bay in the Philippines. The Eighth Fleet called the bay home, and Keith was ready to take the penalty for staying on board ship. The officers insisted that the sailors leave. They were lectured on sexually transmitted diseases and issued condoms and put off the ship.

I have listened to other service personnel describe the area, the impossibility of finding overnight housing except with prostitutes, the endless streets of bars and gambling houses. There was Keith, stuck with his integrity, remembering (as he said) "who he was and where he was from." He found that he could take the military penalties for remaining on board ship better than dealing with a world that violated his integrity at every turn.

I was glad to have immediate access to some experienced people from the Philippines, and got an airmail letter off to Keith telling him how to find a Christian service center which became his home at Subic Bay for the rest of his military career.

Well-formed young adults can tell the stories of their own unsinkable strength, often baffled at how they resisted violating the values they embraced. "I'm a little embarrassed at how easy it was to drop my friends off and tell them I would be back later to give them a ride home," they sometimes say.

It is a reflection that occurs often among those whose self-discipline was grounded in strong doses of role identity, competency, connectedness, and leverage on their own futures.

In this chapter we have looked at simple things. Here are ways parents subconsciously interact with children and teens. With a little more intentional investment, we might see a great strengthening of foundations for our young and for the entire social environment in which we have such a great investment.

There is no golden formula to guarantee that parents will be spared the agony of watching children drift into experimentation or even addictions involving alcohol, sex, and drugs. We can, however, now look at large samples of families and the life choices of their children and conclude that there are factors of strong correlation which let us (1) predict which children will be most at risk and least at risk for such patterns, and (2) design intentional family systems that make for healthy children who, in any study of probability, will not be likely to be victims of destructive and compulsive life patterns. We are also impressed with the patterns that show up in those least-at-risk kids who experiment or become involved with alcohol, sex, or drugs. Their integrity tends to shorten their days in destructive behavior. Evidently the diligent parenting of Prov. 22:6 paid off in the famous parable of the Prodigal Son who "came to his sense, [and] said, I will set out and go back to my father.'"

## QUESTIONS PEOPLE ASK

*Q: It makes me very nervous to think that sex role has to be learned from the parent of the same sex. I am a single parent, and what you say frightens me.*

A: Marshall McLuhan left us one golden text worth remembering: "Nothing is inevitable, if we are willing to contemplate what is happening." So take heart. Single parents have double work cut out for them, but it makes it imperative during the child's first ten years, at least, to get the child into significant environments where appropriate and magnetic sex models are available to your children. Churches, clubs, and schools are often good sources for these, but the child deserves to live in the community with impressive relatives who can fill the gap left by the absent parent. Children are preprogrammed to search out and attach when such people are available. I often urge a single parent to do an environmental check to see who will be there during the childhood and adolescent years. See my comments about how the poles shift at the onset of pubescence in the chapter "Parents and Children for Each Other" in *Bonding*.

*Q: I'm baffled by the self-discipline thing. Our thirteen-year-old doesn't bathe, comb her hair, or brush her teeth. She has a new set of friends about every two weeks because she is so lacking in discipline and basic social sensitivity. How can we get this changed?*

A: You are probably dealing with a child who suffers low self-esteem, which suggests that the role and competency homework is incomplete or may have been disturbed by some family problem. It would be easy to suspect drugs, given these side effects, since a sense of pride is pretty standard equipment on any thirteen-year-old who is into the sexual development agenda of pubescence. By all means get a family systems conference with a psychologist, a pastor, or a social worker who can unravel the potentially complicated roots of this unusual behavior in your daughter.

# 8

## *The Intimate Family*

△

We watched the Johnsons from a distance for several years
and admired them. For one thing, they had brought five children into the world, two daughters and three sons, while we
had the courage only to handle two. We knew the family
because of the reputation of the children who were scattered
throughout the school system where our boys were in school.
Only much later would we get a glimpse into what sort of
motor was driving the family.

Both parents were high energy, competent folks, easily
able to handle absolutely any task reasonable among humans.
No wonder the children looked like world-class teens and
were elected to the highest offices in their worlds. Competency, positive regard, mutual respect—these were abundant
everywhere.

A window on that family would see these amazing things.
You could mistake it at times for a chaotic family. With seven
people using the house as Grand Central Station, it was occasionally a bit confusing. Note these hallmarks of the intimate
family:

1. Breakfast and evening dinner were family events, on
   schedule and punctuated by laughter. Liturgies of grace
   opened those meals.

2. Responsibilities were distributed, negotiated, and carried out with virtually no policing. For example, clothing was delivered to the laundry room on schedule, and it was retrieved in individual plastic baskets, to be folded and stored by the owners.
3. No scapegoating or dumping responsibilities on other family members occurred. Neither favoritism nor sloth showed up. Everybody carried a load of responsibility at home, and most did time in the family business. Eventually, during high school, most of them held down jobs for spending money in addition to starring in extracurricular events at school.
4. With all the heavy scheduling and obligations of seven adults living under the same roof, no one turned up missing without reporting in the location and the cause of the delay. This included the parents.
5. High priority automatically went to the schedules that took the entire family to church and saw them all supporting each other at school, in music, and at athletic events where fans were needed.

"You're really into camping," I said one day to Lorie. "Do you enjoy a whole week of sand and wind?"

"We go to the state park," Lorie once told us, "to get some time away from the telephone and just to be with the family. Around here with everybody's friends popping in and out, we really fall behind in building our relationships in the family. Well, I just have to get Ron away because his business simply consumes him if he doesn't get completely away from it for a week now and then. I have to look out for his welfare; he surely won't do it. So I set the dates, make the reservations, and kidnap him if necessary to be sure we get our time together."

Today there are another five families starting up in imitation of the Johnsons' original model. The daughters have established themselves. One is a distinguished multilingual teacher and the other is an attorney. The sons are entrepreneurs, accountants, and world-class consultants. We think we detect the imprint of that original home coming through in what we see of their households.

In four chapters I want to open up the internal structure of typical families. It is clear that relationships in the family—husband-wife-child dynamics—are profound predictors of what families and children are at risk to seduction and compulsive addiction where alcohol, sex, and drugs are concerned. I must first describe ways we can look at those internal dynamics in a household. Remember that our way of evaluating relationships applies equally well in a multigenerational home, a single-parent home, a fully parented home, a blended family. You name it, the internal dynamics will be open to evaluation in any kind of living environment when we look at family systems.

### Family Systems

The use of family systems language to study family structure now adds an older body of research theory to a newly developing systemic cluster of sciences. Math set theory was an earlier sample of systemic approaches. By "systemic" we mean simply that a whole related cluster of factors are all linked together so that when one of them is changed, all the others are affected.

We can see, then, that a systems approach to families would move on the premise that *relationships are so interconnected that no person is an island cut loose from the other persons in the relationships.* Salvador Minuchin, for example, a prominent researcher of families, insists that the thirteen-year-old girl who is brought to therapy because she suffers from anorexia nervosa cannot be treated successfully if she alone is treated. Minuchin says, "We do not have a girl with anorexia nervosa. We have a family which is showing the symptom of the girl's anorexia nervosa—we have an anorexic family."[1]

The systemic approach, indeed, links up with the most profound realities of the universe. A systemic view of biology or zoology, for example, has given us the phenomenon of cloning. These sciences have shocked us with their findings that any cell of any organism contains the entire genetic program by which a duplicate organism may be reproduced. Dennis Gabor's discovery of the hologram, involving, as it does, the reconstruction of whole images in three dimensions from any fragment of the original image, is another instance of systemic science.[2] We are now discovering that even in theology, a formal creed may not be a whole theology, but that a really sound theology is one which is systemic and can be tested by life, by emotions, by hymnody, as well as by syllogisms invented in words almost entirely dependent on mere rational processes and not on systemic reality.

If theology rests primarily on syllogisms or abstract cardinal doctrines, it is only a partial theology. We call these abstractions "systematic theology"—that is, we have congealed out of God's actions, relationships with people, and human articulations of the revelation of God a distillation of events and actions that were once fully alive. This is to acknowledge that systematic theology is truth with the life knocked out of it. I have appealed repeatedly for us to respect systematic theology, but to recognize that it is only partial. I have urged at the highest levels that we set ourselves to generating a systemic theology. John Wesley, for example, never wrote a systematic theology, although he was systematic about everything he did and earned the nickname "methodist" because of his orderly way of living. I suspect it was his brother Charles's six thousand hymns that kept him from ever freezing his theological ideas into verbal symbols; music always adds a dimension of wholeness to more rational statements. "If you can't sing it, don't believe it," becomes a good caution. Among the major theological movements in the world today, people in the Wesley tradition are likely more holistic, more systemic than most others, especially those that require adherence to verbal codes alone.[3]

### Two Predictors

One of the most helpful summaries of family systems theory has been completed by W. Robert Beavers.[4] For more than forty years I have been trying to keep up with research dealing with families and have done a bit of original research myself.[5]

For more than twenty years I have been attentive to the findings of Sheldon and Eleanor Glueck in their famous

*Unraveling Juvenile Delinquency.*[6] They preceded family systems jargon by thirty years, but in their study of five hundred persistently delinquent boys and five hundred nondelinquent boys who were matched by age, intelligence, ethnic derivation, and neighborhood conditions, they were able to identify five predictors of delinquency and nondelinquency. All of the predictors were grounded in the dynamics of parent-child relationships:

1. Discipline of the boy by the father.
2. Supervision of the boy by the mother.
3. Affection of father for the boy.
4. Affection of mother for the boy.
5. Cohesiveness of the family.

So reliable were the predictors that when they were modified to three that would fit a New York City high-crime urban population, they accurately predicted nondelinquency at a 94.1 percent level and delinquency at a 84.8 percent level in a sample of 300 boys followed from age 6 to 16. The good news even for fractured families comes when you see that those long-term predictions worked with only these predictors:

1. Supervision of the boy by the mother
2. Discipline of the boy by the mother
3. Cohesiveness of the family.

I was grounded in the 1950 research of the Gluecks at Harvard Law School. I had seen similar implications from David Ausubel's satellization theory of child and adolescent development, grounded in his *Theory of Adolescent Development* from 1954. Now, after sorting through Beavers's work, Minuchin's reports on his approaches in family systems therapy, and Nick Stinnett and John DeFrain's unique analysis of thousands of strong families and their systemic structure,[7] a significant truth occurred to me. All these people so committed to creating healthy families identified two basic features of family relationships that seemed worthy of study by themselves. Most of the characteristics of various family systems seemed to have their roots in these two factors.

1. How high or low is the value of the person, adult or child, male or female?
2. How widely is responsibility distributed among the members of the family, adult or child, male or female?

*High value of the person* looks out for each individual person's comfort, preferences, rights, and privileges, and goes in defense of protecting the person. High value shows up in camaraderie, good humor, affirmation, and celebration at the achievement of other people. It deals with conflict quickly and cleanly, focusing on the issues and sparing the person a demeaning assault.

*Low value of the person* shows up in placing self-interest ahead of any consideration of the rights or privileges of other people in the family. This low end of the scale also commonly resorts to ridicule, sarcasm, and profane or obscene language when speaking to or about other people. It is also characterized by violence and abuse.

*High distribution of authority* sees decisions made from data collected from several people and power distributed among all participants.

*Low distribution of authority* indicates a system in which one person controls the family, and members of the family are dependent upon those decisions to control their circumstances.

Throughout this and the following three chapters, I will be offering a four-quadrant diagram on which are arranged the two polarities: value of persons and distribution of responsibility. It will be easy to see how various tendencies on these two factors move family relationships toward the quadrants that bring those values together. You will find that the left side of the diagram represents the low to high range of value of persons. The bottom of the diagram charts the low to high distribution of responsibilities.

No family is locked into any one of the four quadrants. Any family is likely to slip around among the quadrants as various tasks engage family members. Stress on the family is likely to diminish the value of the person and the distribution of responsibility axes at the same time and set the scene for a power-brokering brawl. So the grid is only a map, not a diagnostic tool with which to fix blame. As a map, it may serve us as a useful tool to change the family pain by finding ways to show respect for everybody and by spreading the responsibilities of the household onto more shoulders.

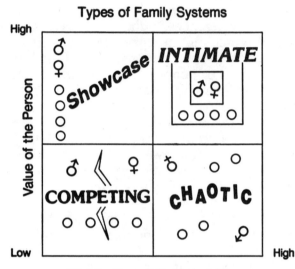

**Types of Family Systems**

Distribution of Responsibility

In this chapter I want to look at the intimate family. This is the name I have given to the family that holds to the high end of the two scales we have watched. They hold to a high view of the value of the person and to the idea that responsibility needs to be distributed to everyone. They value each other simply because they are worth it. There is no other reason that will produce the right stuff. I doubt that any of us could simply say, "I want an ideal family, therefore I will value each person highly." On the second factor, they distribute responsibility all around because they trust each other and know that eventually any one of them will be competent to stand in for any one of the others. So there is no arbitrariness about either of these factors.

What we will see in this chapter is that there is no superficial quick fix to turn any other family system into an intimate system. The only authentic transformation will have to come in a radical conversion of values. Only true believers in each other and in the trustworthiness of one another will win the prizes here.

## The Impossible Dream

We look first at the best of all possible worlds. The intimate family has the highest probability for launching children least at risk to destructive or addictive seductions. This is the toughest model, the intimate family. It goes against the natural grain of human nature. We are bent toward self-service, toward grasping power and control, and toward doing it our way. So the intimate family will be an intentionally chosen domain, where parents and children submit to the discipline of a covenant that hammers out what they intend and what they expect to practice. By contrast, the remaining three kinds of family profiles are the easy family systems, but they are all suffering models. In each of them some member of the family will likely be self-medicating on alcohol or using prescription medication for stress. These systems come at a high price, but they are popular, simple, sometimes even efficient. There is nothing more efficient, for example, than a dictatorship. No time is spent in a dictatorship in training replacements for the dictator; he (or she) expects to live forever. No time is spent in consulting, arriving at a consensus, because one brain makes the decisions and simply announces them. The high-participation model that brings order and not chaos requires time. Hours are needed to coach, facilitate, and train the children and emerging young adults in the family. Then there are the endless huddles, sometimes over meals, to say "We need to make a decision," and lay out the issue and gather the perspective of the full table.

So look at the intimate system with its full stretch to the value of persons and its intentional and systematic distribution of responsibility as illustrated on page 118.

Here are people devoted to each other, without playing favorites, having no tolerance for any kind of cutting or cynical harassment at anybody's expense. Here grievances are settled quickly, tears are respected, and loyalty is not blind

## Types of Family Systems

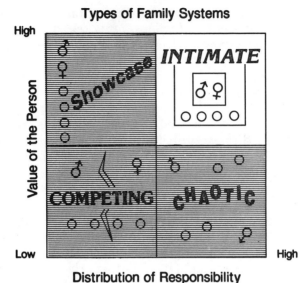

but is based on absolute respect for each other. This family can sustain enormous losses, even the death of a family member, and will not be devastated by unfinished business within the cluster. Grief in competing, chaotic, or showcase families tends to be mixed with the unfinished business of resentment or guilt, so that observable differences show in the grief behavior of close family members. They may be more extravagant in displaying emotion if there is unfinished business, or they may turn to alcohol or sedatives to mask the grief that they know would trigger them out of emotional control.

Here are children who very early picked up the idea that working was fun, that carrying your part of the load was not only a duty, but a very satisfying one at that. You hear almost no talk of chores, but a quick and effective handling of responsibilities that obviously have to be taken care of because so many people depend on their integrity. With each new privilege that comes with maturing, there are new lessons in responsibility. When the driver's license opens the door to the use of the car, for example, the whole array of new responsibilities has to be reviewed. The parent is the coach, not the autocrat. Failing to learn how to handle the responsibilities can lead to some bench time, but only because the rules have to be followed when other people must use the car for other purposes and cannot tolerate failure to return on time or to bring it home with fuel and ready to go again.

Too good to be true, you say? It sounds good and looks good, but it takes enormous energy and intentional commitment to reach the goals you are after—launching competent and responsible adults from your nest.

## Creating the Intimate Family

When we discover truly intimate families or those of their children, we are likely to hear of three trajectories that have led them to the rich relationships of what I am calling the intimate family. Some have received it by inheritance, others through the fires of failure using other models, and a few by sheer intentional commitment to live by the controlling values: respect for persons and covenants of shared responsibility.

"I married into this kind of value system," Mel told me. "My parents had run our family on a pretty authoritarian showcase model, and there were even some of the secret conspiracies you mention in the competing family system. Cindy's family was one of those healthy families that I had admired, but I didn't know the secrets. I could not believe the way they started treating me when Cindy took me to visit them. I am one of those lucky guys who loves his mother-in-law. There has been no power struggle between us. I found that whole family affirming me, respecting me, and making me feel more human and alive than I had ever felt. So I bought into their beliefs quickly and voluntarily. Cindy has had to coach me sometimes, because some of my reflexes are pretty rigid, but I want to repudiate them when I see them rising. I literally married into this intimate model."

Robbie and I represent those who processed a lot of experience, some of it painful, and came into the intimate system through blood, sweat, and tears. We have told our story and even analyzed the stages of a marriage elsewhere.[8] We offered our story but were unable to conclude whether the stages are normally developmental or necessarily so. It evidently was our absolute commitment to the value of each other that eventually generalized as we did our homework on self-worth and saw our two growing sons in truer perspective. That sense of the absolute nonreplaceability of human resources in our family set us up to scramble for ways to launch the boys as more healthy, balanced, respect-based young adults than we had been.

It was easy once we got over our neurotic power games based on our individual insecurities and quit playing the idolatrous game of roles-determine-relationships-and-dictate-family-behavior. The boys suddenly and clearly were capable of much more responsibility and freedom than we had ever thought of giving them. "I trust you to make a good decision, and you are there" was the easy release we gave a college son. "Look after everything for me, I'm going to be out of town for three days," stretched a fifteen-year-old. The days when the drivers' license set them free were high celebration days for us. We knew they were competent to handle the responsibility.

We scrambled with them to support their marriages before they finished college, both because we trusted their judgments about the timing of sexual intimacy and marriage and their readiness for the possible family responsibilities, and also because we knew that they were on a pattern that would soon break them free from our economic support.

The Joys have come into the intimate family system through pain, experimentation, and some turbulence and inconsistency. Especially in the transition from the showcase family system to the intimate one, it was easy to revert to traditional authority patterns. The rewards of intimacy, however, have been so enormous that repentance and apology were easier than going back. The response to our story, both as told in the book and as we share it in a seminar we call "The Seasons of a Marriage," leads us to believe that our developmental story, cemented by an indestructible bond of original respect based on affection, is typical for many people.

One story we hear repeatedly suggests, "Your 'first' marriage and 'second' marriage sounds like mine, but our bond broke under the pressure of the second stage. Now in my remarriage, it had to begin where the old one failed, so our 'blended' family is the first intimate system I have known."

I am beginning to speculate that the horror of divorce, if it is followed by a patient time of reflection and shaking down of values, can set the stage for intentionally entering a new relationship. This must measure up to integrity and mutual respect in a way that many of us are unable to look for in our first time around.

Ed and Sheila wrestled with their relationship late in their dating career. They came to me for premarital counseling and I checked out their family systems background. They had read *Lovers* and said they really wanted to get their marriage started off where ours was now thriving. In three sessions as we talked, it was clear that there was a deliberate conversion from their family-experience bases to the mutual respect and distribution-of-authority system which characterizes the intimate household. In the postmarital sessions that I request, I did the thousand-mile and the five-thousand-mile check-ups, each time inspecting the perceptions of their relationship and the resulting role definitions that were emerging. It appears that this is perhaps the happiest way of transforming, in one generation, the predictable family system that would have emerged through a power brokering and conflicted experience that was inevitable as they married.

## How the Intimate Family Works

The intimate family system is full of communication. This means that meals typically bring the family all together early in the morning and again at the evening. If someone's schedule cuts into the mealtime, everybody suffers. These people are committed to each other and expect to maintain their intimacy through table conversation.

Laughter is the drug of choice in the intimate family. Indeed, the brain releases healing chemicals under conditions that evoke respect-based laughter. These folks do not indulge in cynical, cutting, or caustic humor. They enjoy laughing at themselves. Meals, especially, are times to report funny things that happened on the way to the forum.

I have wanted to call this intimate family the integrity

family. Nick Stinnet and John DeFrain, primary researchers on family issues, call them strong families.[9] Among such families there is a strong tendency for us to find that they include household expressions of religious faith in their conversation agendas. Typical are table grace liturgies and family prayers, involving everyone in the family. "My husband and I were so worried about sex, drugs, and alcohol as our oldest son went into junior high that we talked about it and decided that we could remind the children of who they are and what things are really important if we would take a few minutes each morning to pray before they left for school. We've made it a real 'thing' to simply grab hold of everybody and do our family 'huddle' at the back door before the first family member steps out to face the world. We simply give the day to God and express some of the things we know are going to put us under stress on that day, but we confess that we know that with God's grace we can face whatever comes to us. We got them all launched, and with only minimal skirmishes with crazy stuff. I am sure the prayer time reminded us all that the world outside isn't the real world, after all."

Stinnett and DeFrain report one man's response to the query about what made his business enterprise so successful. He went down the list: hard work, good judgment, treating people right, but he declared that the most important lever on its success was a two-word formula: pray and visualize. When he played out how they worked, it was their way of making the connection between themselves and the great source of life and power that we call God. He reported how he began each day with such prayer as he jogged. Driving to and from work, he said, was critical time for this kind of reflection and visualizing and saying something like, "God, give us your divine guidance and fresh insight in this matter of . . . (whatever was troubling or challenging him at the moment)."[10]

*The Secrets of Strong Families*, an enormous computer-based research project, examined 130 strong and stable families, and yielded amazing profiles, reinforced by data from nearly 3,000 additional families. The survey transcended American borders with 20 percent of the sample coming from outside the United States. Within the United

States, 70 percent were urban and 30 percent were rural families. The families are multi-ethnic, of various economic levels, and include first marriages, remarriages, as well as single-parent households. The strengths were defined by Nick Stinnett at the University of Nebraska and by his colleague John DeFrain of Pepperdine University in California as follows:

1. *Commitment.* Members of strong families are dedicated to promoting each other's welfare and happiness. They value the unity of the family.
2. *Appreciation.* Members of strong families show appreciation for each other a great deal.
3. *Communication.* Members of strong families have good communication skills and spend a lot of time talking with each other.
4. *Time.* Strong families spend time—quality time in large quantities—with each other.
5. *Spiritual Wellness.* Whether they go to formal religious services or not, strong family members have a sense of a greater good or power in life, and that belief gives them strength and purpose.
6. *Coping Ability.* Members of strong families are able to view stress or crises as an opportunity to grow.[11]

The sky is the limit. What kinds of good things can come to a household characterized by absolute mutual respect and by the highest trust in distributing responsibilities?

### Threats to the Intimate Family

Here, we are looking at those unusual families that have intentionally chosen to hitch their household visions to a star. They have managed to do a balancing act of enormous significance: they have reached the golden dream of highest regard for the value of all persons and have distributed responsibility to its widest limits. So here we may do well to note the threats and risks the intimate family sustains.

When priorities shift, the value of persons may slip. Most notable risks involve somebody getting too busy to sustain interpersonal relationships and to maintain the time and emotional investments necessary to sustain the intimate family system. "Daddy doesn't listen to me like he used to," one five-year-old commented after his father's promotion loaded him down with responsibilities he carried in his head during all of his waking hours. "I know Mother really likes her job, but I never see her before I leave for school. She has to sleep late because she gets home late, too." As financial realities change and two or three adult jobs cut into more ideal family scheduling, the intimate family will have to invest some "talking out" time simply to affirm their abiding values and to find ways of recharging everybody's batteries under a new schedule.

The child-bearing and child-rearing years provide the greatest number of booby traps that might sink the intimate family and turn it into a power-brokering deformity of its original self. When we are overextended, overworked, and tired, we tend to revert back to self-centered, even retaliatory moves based on personal power. A hard-working mother and harried children can simply default and throw us back to the showcase family where good old Dad takes over. If he is, indeed, a good old Dad, he will likely acquiesce and take over. So you can see that under the crunch of time constraints, it is easy to lose the collegial, mutually supportive, high participation family system.

It is likely that the intimate family inevitably rests on the highest moral and spiritual platform. We should not be surprised that it is out of the reach of people who are insecure or selfishly dishonest at any level in their lives. We shall expect that should they turn a moral and spiritual corner, the intimate family might show signs of erosion. Thus we can make it our priority to cultivate all those moral and spiritual patterns that make for honesty, integrity, and the affirmation of all that is true and beautiful and good. It is not as simple as saying "go to church" or "be religious." Many religious environments are badly deformed and neurotic, some of them practicing self-centeredness at the institutional level to such an extent that only sinfully self-centered people would know how to cope with them. There are, however, centers of moral and spiritual maturity everywhere, and the strong families tend to find them and to spread the influence of their own wholeness through affiliations with those agencies and churches.

In this chapter I have wanted you to open the door on the most complex and most rewarding family system anyone has studied. I am eager that you begin your adventures toward entering in and bringing off the harvest of high respect for all persons and the widest distribution of responsibilities. With the four models I will discuss, we will not, of course, describe every family you know. These are simply specimen types that explain certain dynamics predictable when given values are present. The bad news is that unless the values change—really change—the system will reflect the deformed values and will remain a deformed and destructive system. The good news is that any deformed system may be transformed into an intimate and strong family system if there is a genuine repentance and disowning of the destructive values that have held a family captive.

It is important, too, to remember that no one person can control a system. Any two or three people can form a confederacy of integrity and move the household toward peace and intimacy. The principles of peace, servanthood, confrontation, and honesty call for openness and respect and for embracing the future, knowing that today is the first day of the rest of our lives and it is time to begin living in a way that honors the value of everybody here.

## QUESTIONS PEOPLE ASK

*Q: I understand very well what you have done. You have reinterpreted the Bible to support your egalitarian marriage and have destroyed a lot of happy homes. Now you are citing naturalistic humanism in turning to family systems research. I am really quite angry at what you are doing to Christian families.*

A: Robbie and I urge you in *Lovers* to take your time. Look inward to your own needs for control and dominance. Search the Scriptures. Pay attention to the Creation—essentially what the social sciences are doing when they

make observations about family dynamics and how they relate to putting children at risk for seduction into drugs, alcohol, and premature sexual intimacy. I am now fifty-nine
years old. I suspect you are something less than that. Sub-
tract your age from mine. You have that long to work out
your own conclusions about God's order for husbands, wives,
and families. There is no hurry. I was past fifty before my
relationships deteriorated sufficiently for me to go in search
of a better way of focusing all of reality: revelation, Creation, and daily experience. So you have plenty of time, I
suspect.

*Q: Have you always known about this kind of mutual re-
spect and high distribution of responsibility family arrangement? I never heard of such a thing. I admit it sounds good,
and I think my wife and I have instincts that lead us to say it's
true. Why haven't we heard about it? In our church we were
never taught this kind of a model at all, although I can see it in
the teachings of Jesus and in the original Garden marriage.*

**A:** No. Robbie and I tell the story of our awakening in
*Lovers*, largely through painful experiences. We suspect that
most of us come to the reconstruction and the discovery
through pain. In our case, we were so committed to placing
our lives under Jesus and Scripture that we went back to both
to ask the really urgent questions about relationships and
about our marriage. You are right. The churches have done
very little to give us a viable model for high respect, high
responsibility marriages and family patterns. I hope many
people will rise up to show us the way.

# 9

## *The Competitive Family*

$$\triangle$$

It was a few minutes past midnight when Carl let himself into the house with a sleeping three-year-old girl in his arms. Nan, the girl's mother was livid.

"You do this one more time, and I'll have the police on you for child abuse," she shrieked, awaking Ginny.

The pattern was typical. Carl had taken Ginny after the evening meal saying he was going to drop in on his Uncle Bill to play dominoes. Once in the pickup, he told Ginny they were driving into Greensburg for a "party." The party was always the same. Ginny would sit with him in the bar for a couple of hours, then he would carry her to the pickup and tell her to lie down and go to sleep. He would lock the doors, leaving Ginny in the darkened parking lot behind the all night grill and bar, and then go back to his friends.

The cover-up was always the same. Ginny loved to go with her Daddy anywhere, so he would say, "Now if you want to go with Daddy, remember to tell Mommy that we went to Uncle Bill's and that when you got tired Uncle Bill let you sleep on his bed."

Nan was not impressed with the deception, but she set up her defenses and enlisted Ginny in a desperate game to outwit his schemes. "Tell Daddy you are too tired—that you want to stay home and go to bed," Nan urged the girl.

Both parents would close their deals with Ginny with "Remember who loves you the most?" Ginny would edit her lines to always agree that the parent asking the question was the favorite one.

In this chapter we are looking at basic dynamics in a family structure I call the competing family. You will have seen the behaviors somewhere, and you will unravel with me the dangerous features of these family relationships. Note that the competing family quadrant on the diagram combines the lowest value of persons with the lowest distribution of responsibility.

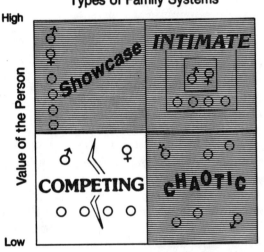

Types of Family Systems

*Distribution of Responsibility*

## Competing Parents

Parents are the core of all family systems, so we may expect the system to be shaped by the parents' behavior and attributes. In this low-low quadrant where the value of persons is low and where the distribution of responsibilities is also minimal, we are looking at a very selfish system. The adults here are the most experienced, of course, and have developed more sophisticated ways of getting what they want when they want it. It may seem ironic to label them as low value of persons since individually they seem to place such a high value on their own desires. This self-centeredness, however, is a dead giveaway that they are insecure, fearful, and suffering from low self-esteem.

If you do any reading on marriage and family relationships these days, you will find several popular writers who say things like: "Of course, husband and wife have the same value, but they serve different functions." Read carefully as you work through their models; functional views of people are clues that the value of persons is relative. If persons have different values, then functionalism will dictate that all decisions be based on the functional values of the people involved. Infanticide, abortion, euthanasia, and indifference in the face of poverty, famine, and starvation are all grounded in relativism based on function. Applied to marriage and the family, the idea is clear: shape up or you're gone. You will see that all kinds of abuse rest on the opposite of God's premise in Ephesians 6 where Paul warns fathers both to be patient in disciplining their children and in governing their slaves. There are no distinctions with God; He loves them equally.

Both Carl and Nan were using Ginny in the anecdote that opened this chapter, a story based on actual events in a family close to me. While Ginny was simply a low-value pawn in one sense, the instrumental use of the daughter only revealed how devalued both parents' views of themselves were. This low view of themselves gets telegraphed to all other human beings, but no one sees them lower than do the members of the household. When Jesus articulated the connection between self-respect and the respect for others, that is, "Love your neighbor as you love your self," he likely was cautioning that self-esteem is a boomerang. With whatever self-respect we have we will reach out to regard others in the same way.

The competitive family is simply a dangerous place to be, since both parents tend to display low self-esteem. This predicts that the children will be the targets of playing out their frustration with themselves. If the father has a bad day, then the children had better beware. If mother is out of sorts, it is a good time to sneak quietly around the house.

The really explosive dynamic, however, shows up as the parents compete for affection and power. Their romance and later sexual behavior will tend to have been characterized by bargaining, games, flare-ups, making up, and apparent reconciliation. When we say that they fight like children, we are insulting childhood. These adults are not simply and naively egocentric, they are egomaniacs who have grown up demanding their own way, often manipulating their own parents and everyone in sight to dominate and control their environments. They have developed a life pattern by which everything has a price. If they are nice to you, you will have to pay. They maintain at least a mental balance sheet on who owes them one. So the marriage is a seesaw of competing balance sheets, each trying to get one up on the other.

Since male dominance is the culturally accepted structure for the family, the wife may give tacit approval to his superior rank, but she tends to use her considerable cunning to outfox him. As the two women in the cartoon "B.C." decided: "Of course we will let our men dominate us. But then we will nag them into submission."

Stress is often terribly intense in the competitive family. Some family member will likely resort to alcohol to mask the pain of low self-value and the guilt of so shabbily treating other members of the family. Often this is the mother's self-medication for the anxiety she suffers, but typically both adults abuse alcohol, using it for escape or to bolster the ego prior to another foray in the search for new triumphs.

It should not surprise us that children of such alcohol abusers themselves see drinking as a means of coping and often use it early. It is not uncommon for children of alcohol-abusing parents to declare that they will never touch the stuff, only to discover in early adulthood that they have, in fact, turned in desperation to alcohol to help them through some life crisis.

## Family Conspiracies

When affection and power are the big stakes over which the parents are competing, children become pawns on the chessboard of the family system. The affection game is called, "Do you love me best?" It tends to be played by each parent against the other. So special favors, comforts, and rewards are doled out to guarantee the special status they seek to buy. Punishment is often deferred to the other parent to alienate the child from that parent through a tattletale routine which characterizes the spouse as a mean person.

Behind closed doors the competing parent will conspire with the children to keep secrets from the spouse. The flimsiest of excuses are given. Mothers frequently warn children that Daddy would be angry and maybe violent if they told him. Fathers frequently say that Mommy shouldn't know because it would hurt her feelings and she couldn't handle it. Both are lies, of course, and paint the parents as weaklings, unable to face reality.

In such a system, of course, if you do not cooperate you are punished. Such families tend to indulge in a great deal of scapegoating behavior in which a noncooperative person is blackballed so as to be shunned and mocked by both polarities in the competing family. Scapegoats are arbitrarily chosen to bear the brunt of any failure on the part of someone else. So there is abundant scapegoating material available, given the adversary positioning of the parents, the need to reward compliant children, and the high level of deception going on. One more lie by which blame is falsely fixed on a noncooperating child is of little importance in the minds of the competitive family members. Indeed, the scapegoat victim may even agree that it comes with the territory of existing family relationships and games.

## Graduate Con Artists

What emerges at once is the fact that the competitive family system is training children to deceive and to lie with high stealth. They have learned the art from both parents, along with the reasoning to accompany not telling the truth to the only people on earth who deserve to know. These are the ones who can be expected to understand and to support the child through tough times triggered by poor choices.

The competitive system tends to turn out preteen shoplifters and children with tendencies to cheat or steal almost routinely. This will tend to happen even with children from households where there is no economic stress and even where there are generous allowances or opportunities for the child or adolescent to earn spending money. It is not easy to say whether this bent toward theft is rooted in the deceptive family system or whether it is simply a wider by-product of egomania that has been seen as the "adult way." If so, then as the child moves out of the house and into social contact, the rule of thumb to follow is simply this: If you want it, scheme any way in the world to get it. They have celebrated with scheming parents upon successfully duping the other parent, so now they find it easy to celebrate egomania conquests privately: they have a secret of their own.

The competitive and scheming family tends to breed high competition in the children as well. Coaches will have to discipline them for playing "dirty," since the moral code of the cheating family moves into the arena and the only consideration is whether the player can get away with it. The collegiality and cooperation that gives us much of the pleasure of organized sports is sabotaged by raw, self-serving, cheating competition. Since the human race is predisposed to self-centeredness, these personality characteristics are among the easiest to cultivate and establish. If this egomania is not confronted during childhood, it is extremely difficult to confront in the adult years.

What shows up so visibly on the basketball court or football field appears in interpersonal relationships as well. However warm they may seem in establishing friendships, friends are friends only if they are useful. A functional or an instrumental value is placed on relationships, and the value is in direct relationship to how much the person furnishes in terms of payoff. The friend may provide social leverage, comradeship, financial ticketing, liquor, or sex. The painful moral fiber shows itself everywhere.

Note that these characteristics are grounded both in low value of persons and in low distribution of responsibility. A further expression of both finds expression in violent profanity and generally obscene language. The urge for power and control tends to evoke putdowns of eternal proportions with their damnation declarations. The devaluation of persons assaults all ears everywhere with obscenities. You will sometimes detect an air of eagerness to shock nice people by turning the air blue. More often, these arrogant tyrants are simply declaring what they believe to be true of the entire human race: all humans are liars, thieves, pimps, and whores, and they would use the same language if they were honest. In this attitude we can see how they assume that everyone else suffers from the same low sense of self-esteem that they do.

### Intercepting the Competitive Family

This is the family that is, among all of the four we will look at, the most difficult to reach. Indeed, so long as the family is functioning, any attempt to confront or to rescue a scapegoat victim is likely to be met with the full arsenal of deception and accusation, even violence. Touch one of these families as an outsider and you may be surprised at how quickly your confrontation triggers their solidarity. By some measures, more than 90 percent of all homicides occur when one family member kills another. The remaining numbers must be heavily weighted toward police and other victims who intervene in family squabbles, only to become the targets of their combined violence.

There seem to be two strategies that work well in providing some degree of hope for the members of the competing conspiratorial family. All families have occasional crises that require social contact. These include any illness or emergency that requires hospitalization or the death of a member of the family. At such times, they are most vulnerable to support, even intimate care-giving. When that support and care are given unconditionally and uncritically, there may even be a visible awakening of a hunger for a better way of life. So such a wedge into the competitive family may be kept in place with very effective results for the entire family. We have to remember that abuse in any system tends to form its own kind of bond. Effectively intercepting a competing system during a time of members' grief may pull a whole tribal group toward healing and grace.

Youth ministers, teachers, and especially coaches are sometimes able to provide an outside link to a world of honesty and integrity that will attract a young member of a competitive family to adopt a different way of life. The years from twelve to fifteen are especially open to alternative models outside the family.[1] The surrogate or adopted parent figure may find the young teen very ready to adopt not only new rules for living, but new values all around. If this transformation is accompanied by a religious conversion in which a new community is formed, this provides a launching pad for adulthood much like that of an admired family. The family member may indeed establish a healthier home than that from which he or she came.

I must caution you, however, that the risks are very high in such intervention. Most children will bolt and return to the high payoff of the self-centered lifestyle learned in the competitive family. You should expect the wrath of the remaining family members if you are overly aggressive in recruiting children or teens away from the family. Indeed, the ethics of such recruitment have to be weighed carefully since the use of psychological coercion even in the service of the highest good must eventually be judged by the most rigorous standards of righteousness and justice, where it is never written that the end justifies the means.

Such intervention or evangelism is itself reduced to competing status and reveals its motives to move on low value of the person and on low regard for the distribution of authority. Functional evangelism, church planting, and appeals for financial support are quickly and transparently visible everywhere. They are perhaps only more visible in the religious communities than in the political and business arenas because every faith system is grounded in a sense of justice and righteousness that should have corrected the tragic distortion before it hit such grand proportions.

In this chapter I have wanted you to look at a family system that is repeatedly polarized over struggles for power, and in which persons are regarded largely as objects. I have pointed out some of the painful curriculum of such a polarizing family, and have indicated how baffling it often is to try to intervene, to bring some health and order to such a system. I have also identified some strategies that sometimes can bring hope and healing to such families and to individual members of the troubled family system.

## QUESTIONS PEOPLE ASK

*Q: Isn't there some competition in every family? I don't think my household acts this way, but I see some of this in the way I behave sometimes as a parent.*

A: Exactly. All of us, since we are fallen human beings, have a central tendency to serve ourselves, to be egomaniacs. The fact that you can see this pattern, describe it, and ask your question, however, is the best evidence of all that you *can* do something about it. All idols lose their power when we can call their names and repudiate their right to dominate us. When Jesus said, "You get behind me, Satan!" it was a clear sign that he had met the enemy and could describe him. It is a pattern worth using. So, welcome to the human race. All of us are capable of indulging in power plays—and all of us suffer from low self-esteem—so in our worst moments we are surely capable of pulling off a competing strategy. The people who are most dangerous are the ones who have no awareness that they are operating out of those low-value power motivations.

*Q: I really resonate with what you have described, and I think I have escaped from just such a family. I married before I was twenty, and my wife's family has become my real family. I adopted them emotionally even before we were married because they were such a positive group of people, and I feel sure that my wife has healed me of my low sense of self-worth. I sometimes slip back into the reflexive behavior I saw all during my years at home, but today I don't feel trapped or like it is inevitable that I will be a competing father and husband.*

**A:** Wonderful. You have obviously been delivered from a lifelong recycling of competitive family relationships. You are proof that there is no absolute determinism in any theory. A theory is only the best way to explain the dominant findings, and never accounts for every case. We often refer to your kind of case as an exception to the rule, but there will always be these wonderful exceptions because grace and hope are alive in the world and your own dream of a better way was met by your dream of a good woman. Your case is like most of those who are delivered from tragic family systems. I suspect that love and marriage are the great delivery plank over which most people come to wholeness. Indeed, the same research that shows the years of twelve to fifteen to be vulnerable to a value shift shows that a second soft spot occurs in the early twenties—exactly at the time when most love-and-marriage deliverances would be occurring.

# 10

## *The Chaotic Family*

△

In *Haywire*, the lovely and tragic story of her famous family, Brooke Hayward describes the losses of a family that, in many ways, fits our criteria of a chaotic family. They were aristocrats in the fast lane. Her mother was Margaret Sullavan, a throaty-voiced actress, the idol of Broadway and movie audiences. Margaret was also the idol of Henry Fonda, William Wyler, Jed Harris, and Leland Hayward. Lois Gould in *The New York Times Book Review* said Margaret Sullavan "wanted most of all to be a perfect mother—and she tried too hard."

Leland Hayward was Brooke's father, of course. He was the "Toscanini of the telephone" who made million-dollar deals for people like Greta Garbo, Ernest Hemingway, Judy Garland, and Lillian Hellman. It is said that he taught Fred Astaire how to dress. Katharine Hepburn once called him the most wonderful man in the world. Yet he never quite heard what his children were saying.

*Haywire* ends with Brooke cradling the head of her dead father. She had missed being there when her mother died and when Bridget, her sister, took her own life. Her brother Bill, largely incapacitated and in a psychiatric hospital, was all she had left.

Now, holding the heavy dead weight of her father's head in her arms she surveyed his body, now so much smaller, already losing its warmth and growing rigid. As she bathed his face with her tears, she imagined him traveling through space faster than the speed of light:

> Where were Bridget and Mother at that very moment, I wondered, reaching out to him over the edge of some distant star? What address should I write in my telephone book after the name "Hayward, Leland"?
>
> My tears drenched his face, glazing it like ice. . . . I wept for my family, all of us, my beautiful, idyllic, lost family. I wept for our excesses, our delusions, and our inconsistencies; not that we had cared too much or too little, although both were true, but that we had let such extraordinary care be subverted into such extraordinary carelessness. We'd been careless with the best of our many resources: each other. It was as if we'd taken for granted the fact that, like our talents and interests and riches, there would be more where *we* had come from, too; another chance, another summer, another Brooke or Bridget or Bill.[1]

## Look Out for Yourself

In our effort to identify families by the two critical factors in our family systems diagram, we are now looking at families that tend to rate low on the value of persons. This means that the parents are suffering from low self-esteem. They likely have met and used each other all the way into a marriage that has a pattern of seeing all people as objects. So they, more than any other family system, tend to show off their babies as objects that they have made. As the children grow up in the house with them, they may toss out oblique challenges that the children may either resent or may try their hardest to live out. "I hope I live to see the day I see my son playing for an NFL team," one such father kept saying while watching Monday night football.

The chaotic family falls in the lower right quadrant of our chart because it rates high on distribution of responsibility. We would expect that high distribution to have significant merit, but since the persons are devalued, we get a full spectrum spread of responsibility through the negligence of the

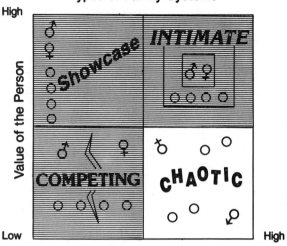

Types of Family Systems

Distribution of Responsibility

parents. This is a default system. So the message arrives early, "Look out for Number One."

The chaotic family appears in all social and economic levels. The effects are the same, too: virtually unpredictable. If you have never lived in such a home or seen one in action, try to imagine what is going to happen when:

1. No meals are served. If there is food in the house anyone may dip in and fix a snack or pack a lunch.
2. No one sets the alarm and coordinates the launch to get children off to school and adults off to work.
3. Laundry is not coordinated or done regularly.
4. No parental support is available for school or other outside opportunities that require an adult sponsor.

In this chapter I want you to look at both father and mother patterns and to trace the wide spectrum of things that tend to happen to children of the chaotic family. Then we will look at ways such a family may come to inner healing. Finally we shall point to some ways those of us who care might intercept a family or at least an occasional member and bring them to higher regard for themselves and for other people.

### Abdicating Fathers

Remember that both parents bring God's first curriculum to a child. Laying aside all stereotypes, fathers and mothers bring order and predictability to a home. Most families are organized around a work schedule that demands regular patterns of sleeping, eating, leaving, and returning to the home. Where wealth or poverty prevail—at either extreme—there may be no work schedule. The cycle of parties among the wealthy tends to be matched by the cycle of socializing by the unemployed, although the environments are quite different.

Fathers can set up the chaotic family by two extremes. First, their influence is governed by the priority they give to work. This can lead to multiple jobs or workaholic devotion to a single job. It can default the father's relationship. If he is self-employed, an entrepreneur, he is likely to be absorbed in starting his business, and the start-up often stretches across twenty or thirty years. Then the "cat's in the cradle" and the little boy has turned out just like Dad.

Second, at the other extreme is the father who is married to happy hour while en route home or after first showing up at home. In the case of the out-of-work father, the depression or its twin terror, alcoholism, may absorb him at home or with his buddies. So with either the workaholic or the depressed or alcoholic father, predictability is gone and an important part of father's basic gift to the children is evaporated, namely, faithfulness to schedule and pattern of performance are not developed as a part of the children's fabric of human life.

In between are the dozens of patterns by which the father is neither predictable: the source of support, nor affection and care. Irregularity, absence, self-centeredness when he is on site, all these distort the world of normal and healthy human existence.

At one level it would be easy to describe such a man as a jerk. He is so consumed by his own self-satisfaction that he deforms the choicest gifts of all: his children. At a deeper level, such men are to be pitied. Their shattered self-esteem sends signals of desperation, fear of failure, a need to prove something to the world. Their typical macho abhorrence of helping to give necessary support and care to child-rearing tasks may seem studied and rehearsed, and indeed may have been learned in their own childhood homes. They are empty, hollow men and may be quite unaware that they are failing their families. If they do sense what they are doing to destroy their families, the sense of failure tends only to drop them deeper into their addictions.

### . . . and Mothers

Mothers are also God's first curriculum for children. The core experience of mothers is typically a sense of security, warmth, and centeredness. This is true of working mothers, stay-at-home mothers, even mothers of those of us who are ourselves grandparents. Mother means "at peace" and "home."

On the phone to his mother at work, our thirteen-year-old grandson, seated at the lunch table with Robbie and me, responds to the question we did not hear, "Where are you calling from?" "Grandma's house." This centeredness is displayed when every football player with a chance to mug at a television camera calls out, "Hi, Mom!" It is a credential earned through simple mothering, especially through nurturance and primary care that the early weeks necessarily load onto a mother. Give us a little time with our mothers and we know the world is going to keep moving forward. Occasionally a mother damages that center pole for her children. When the young child loses that fixed point at which affection, security, and sustenance come into focus, we can predict a wide range of long-term problems. Look at what happens to mothers who are part of the problem in the chaotic family.

As with men, a mother may put priority on a career or on soap operas and cheap wine—and produce about the same effects as a dysfunctional father does in a family system. So we are not surprised to see chaotic families among entertainers and among blue collar, stay-at-home mothers whose boredom and selfishness cause them to tune out the world of their children and their households.

Depression, overeating, alcohol, and tobacco show up as symptoms of low self-esteem and frustration. Add cocaine and marijuana to the arsenal of escapist chemicals and we can see the same wide spectrum of the social and economic scale crashing down on all of us. The chaotic family may turn up anywhere at all. The busiest career mother instinctively attends to her children's health, nutrition, and cleanliness, thus establishing that centered magnet toward which the family turns for security and trust. When she is whisked away for days on end on professional duty or is incapacitated through clinical or alcoholic depression, the chaotic family is launched.

## The Unpredictable Children of Chaos

Here they come, the children of the other-priority parents. Oddly enough, some of the children will rise to the occasion, even assume parentlike roles. Six-year-olds have been known to prepare meals for siblings and parents. Many children of chaotic family systems will make some effort to order their households, but they cannot sustain such high energy over the long term. We can predict that their high need for order is likely to be so assaulted by the chaos that there will be long-term emotional scarring, likely with medical and psychiatric care down the line. Or they will reach out for other models and mentors, from which to draw strength and construct their visions. The children of chaos who survive with health and productivity have consistently found a surrogate parent somewhere. Sometimes it was a teacher, a coach, a neighbor, or a minister.

Other children simply fall apart emotionally, lacking the inner structures to cope with the absence of external structure. They tend to experience failure early and for long periods of time. The failure will be easy to spot at school, of course, but their social skills and work habits are typically retarded, so the failure that hurts the most is social ostracism or abuse.

Occasionally we see a star born out of the chaotic home.

The story of the heroic kid who got his first job as bank janitor and became president of the bank typically gives us a glimpse of a chaotic home as we survey the childhood. These self-made people tend to become workaholics, often establishing fine reputations. As adults, they shudder to see how slim their chances were to have made it so well. They shudder, too, to see the cyclones of mental illness, alcoholism, and other addictions sweep through their sibling family.

At Harvard Law School many years ago now, Sheldon and Eleanor Glueck studied the characteristics of delinquent and nondelinquent boys. A critical difference, they found, was a predictor they used called "family cohesiveness." The highly cohesive family has at least one meal together every day, celebrates birthdays, and takes vacations together. The low cohesiveness group ate virtually no meals together, observed no celebrations, and vacationed separately if at all. The polarities on that critical predictor were obviously opening up what we see today as the chaotic family system.[2]

### Intercepting Chaos

Unlike the competing family, the chaotic family is easy to invade. It is virtually impossible to connect with the family. While the door may be open to all comers at all hours of the day or night, you would rarely find an occasion to see, much less hold a conversation with the entire family. The exceptions are funerals, weddings, and perhaps a reunion of the larger clan. In their better moments, they appear to be happy, buoyant, often extroverted or laid back and otherwise independent people. Their children tend to be streetwise and out of the house early, though not always caught in the downward spiral of preadolescent streetdom. Because of this early independence, their children are often leaders among their peers. Since they were reared without constraints, they easily lead the pack in experimentation with alcohol, sex, and drugs. The more withdrawn children of the chaotic family may be self-medicating their depression and sense of helpless worthlessness with alcohol or street drugs, but the more extroverted and leadership-oriented ones will seem immune to addiction at this time.

Here, as with the children of the competing system, a charismatic coach, teacher, Sunday school teacher, scout leader, or pastor may be able to toss a delivery line to the child or teen of a chaotic system home. We are likely to miss the more introverted, reclusive children and youth of these families, since they do not sparkle with leadership charm, are less likely to show up with a friend at the church youth gathering, and do not send us signals suggesting that they are interested in the world of normal and healthy families.

There are remarkable cases of people who were thus rescued in the years from ten to twenty. Their stories are the rags-to-riches variety. If they came into significant contact with family systems where mutual respect, family cohesiveness, and highly visible structures, rituals, and support were provided for them, they frequently went on to establish integrity, even intimate families.

In this chapter, I have wanted you to look at the liabilities that follow when parent priorities place self-respect and respect for their spouses and children down the scale behind other self-chosen idolatries. I have also wanted you to examine the bizarre pattern that emerges when the regular patterns of family support such as meals, laundry, and daily rituals are missing. We move now to look at a family system that places a high value on persons, but where a coalition on the power issue has vested it all in one person.

## QUESTIONS PEOPLE ASK

*Q: I think I am a child who came from what you describe as a chaotic family. We had meals together twice a year, literally: Thanksgiving and Christmas. It was every man, woman, and kid for themselves the rest of the time. This was true even during part of my childhood when my mother was not working outside the home. What I wonder is why some of us did so well in that kind of a home and why my sister, for example, has been depressed—officially diagnosed that way—for most of her adult life. Life has been really hard for her.*

A: Two things may help us to focus your sister's case. It is easy to see that you adapted very well. There is little question but that genetic factors exert more than 50 percent of influence on personality structure, so it isn't enough to say that she could have coped if she had tried harder. It seems likely that the extroverted personality may thrive better by keeping feelings and frustrations ventilated, while a more introverted person tends not only to turn inward, but to become negatively fixated on her own situation. She is more likely, perhaps, than you, to blame herself for the fact that life is not more ordered and meaningful than it is turning out to be. Add to this the fact that both the competitive and the chaotic family systems tend to select a scapegoat on which to unload a lot of blame and shame. If she came under that sort of load, and if she was also nicely introverted, you can see that she might have suffered maximum damage over the most impressionable and formative years of her life. Build a bridge to her and give her the affirmation she may not have received long ago. It sounds like you have some positive emotional money in the bank to share.

# 11

## *The Showcase Family*

$$\triangle$$

Here they are, our final family system. The showcase family—the family the way it is supposed to be. Or is it?

Elvin and Laura were hard-working folks. They planted their feet in the soil, but it might have been in the suburbs. They were lovers, high-energy, hard-working people. The children started coming until there were, in this sequence: Charles, Genevieve, Otto, Geraldine, Anita, and Evelyn. They came all within fifteen years, so the house fairly rang with the sounds of childhood and the teen years.

Elvin and Laura had met, actually, in the peak of a religious revival that transformed their hometown. When they married, they found property and managed to buy a whole array of new buildings, including a rambling two-story farm home. Their home, they determined, would be a Christian home.

On the farm it is easy to distinguish men's work from women's work, and there is plenty of both kinds. The roles determined the relationships, I'm afraid, more by accident than by intention. "That's woman's work!" became a quick retort if one of the boys was asked to deal with household food details, including the killing and preparing of chickens for the summer table. "That's man's work!" separated the

146

wife and daughters from the farming operation, even when an extra driver was needed.

The children grew up to be beautiful young adults, popular at school, but more than half of them established reputations in the fast lane. They seemed more at risk to substance abuse and sexual activity than anyone could have predicted, especially since they grew up with daily family prayers at the breakfast table and with required church attendance at Sunday school, worship, youth meeting, evening service, and Wednesday night prayer meeting. How could such a fine training program fail to deliver the goods of moral responsibility and deep Christian discipleship? People watched them pull away from where most good kids were headed. They scratched their heads and wondered what had got into them?

Surprisingly enough, the showcase family is often flawed at the core, and the children are put at risk to indulgences of many kinds. The apparent reasons for that vulnerability are so subtle as to be almost overlooked. As a teen, I had no hint why some of my friends slipped into the wild stuff. Today, family systems research may have turned up a clue to help us understand and move toward prevention if we care enough.

In this chapter, we need to see what happens when a family is organized around a high value of persons but that value is distorted by a low distribution of responsibility. The deformity of this contradiction in values gives us what has been estimated as the predominant model of the family today. Some estimate that it accounts for nearly two-thirds of all households. You will hear high-value-of-persons people justify the low distribution of responsibility in consistent rhetoric:

Well, somebody has to have the final say on everything.

Everybody knows that General Motors or the Army would fall apart if there were no chain of command.

I think a husband and a wife have equal value, but they cannot have equal authority. They have different functions. Men are to be heads and women are to submit.

Man and woman are created equal, all right, but God requires the woman to live in submission to the man.

No one can serve two masters. That's why you cannot have equal authority between the parents.

Elmer and Laura, both nicely extroverted and energized people, hammered out their roles and conformed their relationships quite voluntarily to a chain-of-command model. People never saw conflict between the parents. They seemed eagerly to embrace their roles. It was the children who seemed to suffer. In this chapter we will explore the probable reasons for their vulnerability to the fast lane.

## The Seducing Leverage

Now picture where we are in our family systems grid. The showcase family rates the value of the person very high. Everybody agrees, at least on paper, that this corporation must have only one head. So the distribution of responsibility axis shoves us into the top, left-hand quadrant of the model:

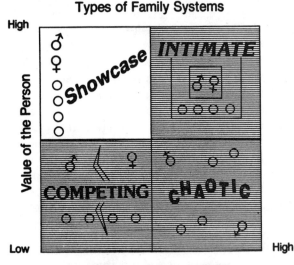

The research suggests that the chain of command does not always hang from a power position occupied by the father, although most do—at least on paper. Some families are organized around a strong mother who exercises virtually all authority. One of the more amusing versions of the dominant woman comes through with her assertion: "Bud knows he's in charge at our place, but I have a terrible time getting him to do what he knows is right."

There are others that are controlled by a powerful person in a previous generation—typically a grandparent whose enormous influence casts a shadow everywhere. In most cases the grandparent is an occasional visitor, supervisor, evaluator, critic, and source of gifts and praise. In rare cases the significant controlling person is even dead, yet casts a powerful influence, like a spell, on the family.[1]

"Your Grandmother would never approve of your dressing that way" is a typical indicator of this rare but powerful absentee authority that invades the family.

What happens in this amazing family system is that the arbitrary decision to verticalize responsibility and to vest full authority in a solitary head actually transforms an otherwise healthy family system into one which devalues everybody but the top person. When this happens, we have relative values placed on various persons in the family. We bump into a contradiction best expressed, probably, in the famous line from George Orwell's *Animal Farm:* "All animals are created equal. But some are more equal than others."

## More Equal Than Others?

In the showcase family there are a pair of traditions that look so good that we have enshrined them in religious and in national secular celebrations: Women are seen as goddesses, to be adored, worshiped, protected, made into symbols of beauty, tenderness, and nonwork objects of artistic leisure. Men are seen as warriors, protectors, competitors, wage-earners, and winners of women. Women and men, of course, are much more than those things, but even when women must do women's work it is calculated to limit their domain to the domestic side, and there the showcase traditions proliferate again: Women are the food preparers, servers, and homemakers. Men are the laborers who come home to be pampered.

I said the flaw was a subtle one. It is so hidden as to be

entirely missed unless we magnify it to examine it. Consider these questions: What will a girl assume about the value of a woman if she sees her mother adored, reverenced as a soft and lovable object of her father's affection, but sees her at the same time having no influence on the family's fortunes beyond the domestic side? What will a boy assume about the value of a woman if he sees his mother embraced as a love object but later ignored as if she were an incompetent, childlike adult?

What will a girl assume about the value of a man if she sees her father as a man whose word is law, nonnegotiable even with his wife, her mother, and whose every wish within the house is both his wife's and his daughter's command? What will a boy assume about the value of a man if he sees his father always having his own way, effectively silencing the boy's mother and reigning supreme?

That is enough. There you have the subtle curriculum that scrambles many children. We get deformed young adults, and the messages come through in their behavior.

### Daughters of Showcase Families

The young woman's view of herself tends to run along stereotypical lines that are affirmed both in the popular culture and in much of the religious community:

1. I want a man who can think for me, decide for me, and take care of me.
2. In my search, I will assume that dependent role, and will rehearse it in my dating and other social contact, giving off the signal of my need for an authority figure and his pampering.
3. I am the lucky sex. I don't have to take initiatives, I can be coy, playful, and reject the wimps and the ugly ones until I get the man of my dreams.

You don't have to be a prophet to predict where such a view of herself is going to take her as she begins to move in today's social structure. She is exactly the person any self-centered young man is seeking. He will call the shots, she will comply.

She is a good sport, but she is also an easy victim. Seduction into alcohol, sex, and drugs comes much too easily for her.

### Sons of Showcase Families

The young man's view of himself gives us at least a temporarily dangerous man about town. His perceptions match the stereotype of the popular culture and much of the religious community:

1. I am a decision-maker. I am free. If I want it and can get it, I deserve it.
2. What I want is an object of my adoration, not a person, not a thinker, only an art object and a lover.
3. I am the lucky sex. I can take the initiatives, impress them with my masculine skills, going on the masculine prowl, until I find a woman of my dreams who 'knows her place' and fits beside me just right.

Typically the young man gets some of the benefits of his male gender right out of his father's bank account. He often has his own car during high school—his father's way of introducing him to the world of male managerial privileges. You can see that his handsome launching can put a very attractive playboy on the streets by age sixteen. He is above the rules since—by virtue of his male superiority—he is in charge. So moral constraint is a function, simply, of whether you are clever enough to keep your nose clean, to keep your illegal and immoral behavior under wraps.

You can see the dynamics. Young women from showcase families tend to leave the thinking to males. Young males from showcase families assert their preferences and carry out their decisions overriding the woman's point of view. "I know that my boyfriend and I are being too intimate, but I also believe that it is the man's place to make the decisions and it is my responsibility to go along," was the line I got from a college woman. Sexual seduction is especially a threat if it moves simply by the rising male appetite in a young man who has been taught by his models that what I want is right because I am a man. Date rape is frequent among such couples, and marital sex by male demand will continue until male midlife, when his loss of the instant demand appetite is likely to drop him into depression and likely into impotence. These probabilities are based on the logical consequences of a pattern in which his arousal has been on demand and not programmed to intimacy based on respect and a growing relationship. In the damaging vertical dating pattern typical of showcase children, if the man wants pornographic movies or videos, liquor, cocaine, or tobacco as an experimental buzz, the woman has been programmed to go along.

## Deformity and Consequences

Here is the proverbial double standard come to life. However much the young man adores his mother, he sees her as his father's object, playmate, and slave. The young man also sees himself as a lord of the castle and invents adolescent forms of swaggering to impress the ladies. Here come the artificial masculinity markers of conspicuous consumption: drugs, marijuana, alcohol, cocaine, and sex. I call this deformity the Fonzie syndrome in another place.[2] This preoccupation with exaggerated pseudomasculinity shows up in father-absent boys, but also at a very high rate in these *paterfamilias* sons.

The compliant and coquettish young woman syndrome, I have compared to Aldonza.[3] In the early stages the young woman's self-esteem sank to Aldonza's tragic low. Nevertheless, the early signals suggest she is on the road down. Low self-esteem will not have occurred to her on the conscious level, of course, since she feels lucky to have no responsibility at all. At some deep inner level the daughter of the showcase family tends to know that she is powerless and that knowledge often erodes her sense of self. She often curbs her academic performance lest her straight "A" report card should diminish her chances at being perceived as a woman who knows her place. She often begins to overdress and be oversensitive lest she seem to be competing with boys. Her erosion of self-esteem is often visible by the end of high school. If she is not picked up in the first-round draft and into marriage by twenty, she is likely to get into the Aldonza circuit as serious business during the first half of her twenties.

The woman who sees herself as inferior to men in general and eventually to her husband tends to remain, at best, forever a child. At worst, such women deteriorate into restless or depressed women. She tends to turn to prescription drugs to cope with feelings of worthlessness and lack of respect. Some women turn to alcohol and street drugs, but the showcase family image holds most of them to the path of seeking medical attention with the resulting dependence on chemicals prescribed by the family physician. Her addiction of choice tends to be tranquilizers.[4]

While the competitive and the chaotic families tend to see someone abusing alcohol in an effort to deaden the reality of low value of persons, the showcase family is vulnerable to prescription drugs. They are too much concerned with appearance to turn easily to alcohol abuse. This family is overly dependent on physicians, and when the stress shows up in a diagnosis it is easy to accept a tranquilizer to see you through the tough times. The drug of choice is Valium, and these showcase families tend to keep it in the medicine cabinet. Often it is the mother who uses Valium, but fathers under stress sometimes are directed to use tranquilizers or some other prescription drug for hypertension. Interestingly enough all four quadrants have an expressed drug of preference. Valium for the showcase folks, alcohol for the competitive and chaotic families, and laughter as the natural high of the intimate family system.

### Intercepting the Showcase Family

Here may be the toughest task of all. This family looks good, has everything going for it, and knows that it is playing by the book. Religious showcase families can cite chapter and verse to support the vertical, male-command model.[5] In every culture the showcase model appears in some form, and is highly compatible with polygamy and status and role images attached to marriage. Polygamous cultures invariably move on the chain-of-command principle.

The idyllic Mormon family, rooted as it is in an Old-Testament-like polygamous philosophy, is profoundly patriarchal and is so slick in its showcase veneer that its chain of command is offered a sick society as the television model of the best of all family worlds.

Yet a closer look locks its philosophy into Genesis 3 and the curse. The Fall dictates that women are chattel, functional incubators, whose husbands will rule over them, so their obligation is to adore their husbands and live in unilateral submission to them—not in mutual submission as Jesus and Paul dictate. The showcase vertical household is everywhere, not even primarily in societies influenced by Judeo-Christian ideas. The most secular of societies exploit relationships, marriages, and families by the showcase roles and expectations. Even the so-called liberationists complain about male roles in relationships.[6] The human race seems to be intuitively indoctrinated to verticalized marriages and families. Fundamentalist religious groups tend to major on enforcement and articulation of male headship and the chain of command. They wrest some twenty verses from the Bible to make their point, all the while ignoring the overwhelming images and teachings about coregency, joint-tenancy, joint-heirship in Christ, mutual submission, and perfect love.

The vote is unanimous—cross culturally and cross theistically. The showcase family system is normative for humans. Here we confront a terrifying question: Is what is, what ought to be? The naturalistic fallacy may have trapped us into thinking the Fall should be baptized and marketed as God's order for families.[7]

Churches, agencies, and all caring professions tend to hit a brick wall when trying to confront the showcase family. There are cracks in the armor if one looks closely.

Men who know the considerable strength of their wives and daughters often are able to hear the offer to widen their resource base for decision making and shared management. Women who have graciously swallowed their gifts and their opinions are often ready to come out of the closet and stand face to face with their husbands as coregents and joint heirs of God's promise.

Sons who have seen the waste of human potential in their mothers' indentured service, or the lonely positioning of their fathers as they became isolated by demands for omniscience and omnipotence, are ready to consider a richer model for their relationships. Daughters who have caught the vision of being partners, of shouldering their side of the image-of-God tasks in the world are ready for higher and better images of vocation, marriage, and family.

Unlike the competitive and the chaotic families, the showcase family will most likely be intercepted at the conceptual, ideological, and theological level. They are serious about learning, seminars, preaching, and Bible study on the issues. They tend to take Scripture seriously and are often ready to look at literal statements that contradict their unhappy and unreflected traditional view. They are ready to look at alternative models, to listen to the story of men and women who have struggled with roles and relationships and have made the transition.[8]

Young men and women are open to alternate models visible in their high school and college years' environments. Mentors and other admired people cast a long shadow across their present unreflected and virtually instinctual tendency to replicate the universal human tendency toward verticalizing power. Premarital counseling offers an unusual opportunity for exploring expectations for roles and relationships in the marriage, and for assessing present positioning between the couple.

When I spoke recently at a large Christian university, I began by saying that I had been born, reared, and came to manhood with an understanding that in the Creation God had first formed a bachelor, called him Adam, and then later created woman, almost as an afterthought, for the exclusive use of the man. To my astonishment, the gymnasium broke out with applause, whistles, and male voices in a unison cheer.

I went on immediately to say that after I had passed fifty years of age, I discovered that nowhere in the Bible is such an idea taught. Instead, I said, God created man and woman of the same stuff, bone of the same bone, flesh of the same flesh, and gave them dominion, establishing that they were coregents, joint-tenants, and that the Apostle Peter had cautioned men to treat their wives in this way, remembering that they are joint-heirs of God's promise. Peter also said that if men forgot this mutual respect-based relationship, their prayers would not be answered. At that moment, the other half of the gymnasium exploded with applause and cheers.[9]

How do you account for the universal affirmation of the chain of command? It would be too simple to suggest that children learn it from their parents. Theologically it is clear that the showcase family is really the family of the Fall. Original sin evoked God's judgment, two curses, and three sets of consequences. The man and the woman were not cursed, only the serpent and the soil were so addressed. The man and the woman, however, were warned of the consequences that would deform their relationship. To the woman, God warned, "Your desire shall be for your husband, and he shall rule over you." Perhaps that is as comprehensive a cause as we will find. It matches the universality of the phenomenon. Both socially and theologically, we are on a pilgrimage in which we expect to find a way to turn back evil on itself, to be set free by grace.

In this chapter, we have looked at the most normal looking family in the world. I have called it the showcase family because it looks so idyllic. We have had to face the fact that there are hidden values in the showcase family that tend to teach children tragic conceptions of themselves, and we must turn to the intimate family system if we are to reduce the enormous risks in an age of promiscuity. We want to protect our children from unnecessary programming toward vulnerability to alcohol, sex, and drugs.

## QUESTIONS PEOPLE ASK

*Q: I'm finding it really hard to see any other way than the chain-of-command structure for a family. That is the way I was raised and that is the way I'm most comfortable. My husband is good at it, too, and our children feel secure with him as boss, so I gladly support whatever he says.*

A: Join the club. If the majority wins, then the chain-of-command family gets the blue ribbon. There is nothing more efficient than a benevolent dictatorship, and some of us did a pretty good job living up to that title. We simply have to take seriously the ways we are putting our children at risk when we restrict responsibility and thereby damage otherwise strong moral fiber in our children. We are going against the Judeo-Christian vision of coregency, joint tenancy, and joint-heirship in Christ if we stay with the vertical model. You are right. It works.

*Q: Why don't you teach the Bible model instead of your secular models for families?*

A: Robbie and I put together a whole book on the Bible model for families. We called it *Lovers — Whatever Happened to Eden?* We could have written a chain-of-command model book twenty years ago. We were living it out. That was before we studied Scripture and found we were, indeed, living out the Fall, not Creation, grace, or redemption. I have turned in this book to a more narrow subject: how do we reduce the risk of putting our kids at risk for seduction into drugs, alcohol, and premature sex? Those are questions today that have very wide interest beyond the faith community, so this book is the research companion to *Lovers*.

# 12

## *Bonding in the Family*

△

We arrived within a half-hour of Heather's birth. Dorian was sitting up cross-legged on the gurney, still in the hallway outside the delivery room. Mike was beside her, dressed in his hospital greens. They were ecstatic in their joy.

"Oh, you didn't get to see Heather!" Dorian exclaimed. "Mike, go see if you can get her."

I thought, "If this is any kind of a hospital he can't get her." About then, here he came rounding the corner carrying a naked, unwashed baby girl with bright eyes reaching out to take us all in. I was only to learn some five years later about the natural high that characterizes newborns and keeps them wide awake for about three hours, during which time birth bonding occurs.[1]

I had thought, looking at Dorian there with her post partum elation, "Don't you know you are supposed to be lying down, taking it easy, after what you've just been through?" Her total communication sent me clear signals that she was doing exactly what was appropriate—enjoying Heather's wonderful arrival.

"Do you want to hold her?" Mike asked Robbie. It never occurred to me to hold her. It didn't seem right, somehow. She was not yet washed, was streaked with blood from the

158

birthing process, and was nude. Grandmother Robbie, looking into the face of her second grandchild, was entirely uninhibited.

"Did they say it was safe to have her out here in the hallway?" I asked Mike.

"'Just don't keep her too long,' they said." Hospital protocol was different from anything I could have imagined. So for more than fifteen minutes Robbie held Heather, getting in a few stolen kisses, and we let her go.

Today, Heather is almost a teenager. There is still a special bond between Robbie and Heather. Perhaps it would have been there anyway, but I doubt it. One time, when she was about four years old, Heather moved her stool at the breakfast table to be able literally to lean over and touch her grandmother as they sat at the table.

"She's really your girl," I commented as Robbie came to the table. By now we had a second granddaughter, Lesli, Heather's sister. I had not contemplated how my remark might sound to anyone, I was just stating an obvious fact. Lesli leaned forward over the tray of her high chair. She pointed to her own chest and said, looking at me: "I'm your girl, Papaw." And she is. Neither Robbie nor I were at her birth, arriving as we did from Europe and phoning from Kennedy Airport to see whether she was yet born and welcoming her long distance. She has extended to me a special gift. I love to play games with her and I often tell her she is my only blue-eyed granddaughter. Besides that, she has many of the ways and looks of another girl I didn't know so young, her grandma.

Robbie and I were leaving Lexington for a weekend in Pikeville, Kentucky. Justin was barely six months old. He is our truly birth-bonded grandson, now an astonishingly competent young man who blows us away with his mastery level at home and at his Montessori school.

We had the luxury of taking him at six months for his first weekend separated from his parents. They were planning a getaway, and we relished the time with him. I was to be talking about bonding issues in a church-based weekend of seminars.

For about ten minutes it looked as if we might not get

Justin in our car. He was clinging to Mike, his father. There were whimpers of refusal and strong clinging gestures that Mike read infallibly. A few months later when we encountered similar behavior, I made a deal with Mike that we were not going to rehearse the bad-guy role by coming and taking him away from his nicely bonded home, but they would deliver him to us on more neutral turf. That Friday afternoon now so long ago, Mike whispered some magic words in Justin's ear. Justin turned toward me, and I took him into the front seat of the car and strapped him into the centered car seat.

Even today, Mike cannot remember what he whispered to Justin, but we were barely out of the driveway before he leaned toward me, touched my arm and leaned up close to me. It was clear that Mike had verbally transferred a bond to me. That bond has been remarkable. On the occasions when Justin and his sisters Heather and Lesli are overnight guests in my absence, Justin has consistently searched through the entire rambling two-story house to verify for sure that "Papaw is not here." He has often asked several times of Robbie to try to comprehend why it is that I am not at home.

In this chapter I want you to look at the often subtle and spontaneous ways families build indestructible attachment to each other. These lifelong agendas we carry out are evidently rooted in the deepest, intrinsic patterns of our humanity. On the other hand, those delicate instincts are easily blunted, perhaps hopelessly damaged. So in tracing the main lines of these fragile potentialities, I am eager that you identify the possibilities in your own family that may lead to increased quality and grace in all your relationships.

### Conception Bonding

There is a magical chain of bonding which guarantees that the conception of new life *necessarily* occurs within the intimacy of the most powerful human bonding. No one can deny that conception sometimes occurs as a result of rape, even marital rape, or as the consequence of one or both of the partners indulging in sexually addictive and compulsive behavior. Nevertheless the life-chain is designed to begin as the seed is planted by gestures of the most intimate loving.

I suspect that there is a sense in which conception and the formation of a one-flesh product of the sexual union of a man and a woman form the ultimate bonding step. So when I outline the twelve steps of bonding,[2] I frequently am tempted to add step thirteen: conception and birth of the first child. Indeed, marriages without children tend to hit an emotional and a romantic plateau that seems sometimes to be evident even in the emotional and ego development of the adult partners. I speculate that it is the parental gift of life and sharing and investing in the intimate care and responsibility for that child which produce the absolutely indestructible bonds that cement families together.

Selfish love might drive a couple to erect what Sheldon Vanauken and his beloved Davy called the "Shining Barrier" to keep out all alien bonds, including children.

> We raised the Shining Barrier against creeping separateness, that was, in the last analysis, self. We also raised it against a world of indecencies and decaying standards, the decline of courtesy, the whispering mockers of love. We would have our own standards. And, above all, we would be *us*-centered, not self-centered. . . . It was now that we re-examined our doubts about children. . . . In the pattern of modern life, where they became the center for the woman, they were separating. We would not have children.

They went on to include a death pact that would be tested sooner than they imagined. "And so we completed the Shining Barrier," Sheldon writes. "We would die together." C. S. Lewis helped Sheldon and Davy to re-examine the selfish nature of their barrier.

> The Shining Barrier was more than that [simply being true to the sacrament of marriage]. In its Appeal to Love—what is best for our love—as the sole criterion of all decisions, it was in violation of the Law; for what was best for our love might not be in accordance with our love and duty to our neighbor. The Shining Barrier contained an ultimate defiance of God in our resolute intention to die together in the last long dive.

But the Shining Barrier had been breached by God's assault troops, including C. S. Lewis in the van; and we had bent the knee.[3]

Couples may have babies for very selfish reasons, of course, but decisions against parenthood may also be grounded in ultimate selfishness.

So let conception stand both as the bonding extension from the pair-bonding sequence and as the bond that opens the door to let the floodgates of affection reach out to establish the larger family bond.

During the months while the baby is forming, the powerful bonding affection of the couple begins to focus on the coming child. When fetal movement establishes the reality of a new and separate life with separate motion and mind, the attachment accelerates. Who can say what the reciprocal benefits of prenatal-bonding may be? David and Sarah Baldridge began to sing to their unborn child when movement began. They decided to sing one song repeatedly. It was the lullaby, "Jesus Loves Me, This I Know." For reasons that seem magical, but may be rooted in the sound patterning in the mind of the unborn child, their baby seemed always to be comforted by the song. Robbie once accompanied the Baldridges on a two-hundred-mile trip to join me at Evansville, Indiana. During the time little Benjamin was uncomfortable and fretful, but could always be quieted by either parent simply starting up the imprinted prenatal lullaby.

Women who abort a pregnancy are always vulnerable to grief that is grounded in the loss of the life. Those women are especially affected who have been bonded by fetal movement. So the most positive bonding effects are likely to be those which see both parents attending to the prenatal chamber, making tactile and auditory contact with the coming visitor. The first nine months of human life are indeed rich in bonding possibilities.

### Parental Bonding

Elsewhere I have unfolded the amazing saga about the first two and a half hours of life and the mystery we are coming to call birth bonding.[4] It is enough here to note that when both the father and the mother can be present at the birthing and can have significant touch, facial, and voice contact with the newborn there appears to be a magical attachment that works both to bond the child to each parent and to bond each parent to the child. A side benefit, of course, is that the two adults are bonded to each other in a most powerful way.

Parental bonding goes forward continuously and in many cases without interruption for all of life. There is, perhaps, no more moving tradition than the one that has Mary, the mother of Jesus, seated and rocking the body of her dead son at the foot of the cross. I have seen Michelangelo's *Pieta* and the lovely *Pieta* that graces the entrance of The Valley of the Fallen south of Madrid. Recently I saw the Easter pageant, "He Wore My Crown," at Southland Christian Church near our home. Suddenly I broke into a cold sweat as they removed the body from the cross and a strong man placed the limp body of our central actor into the lap of the woman playing the part of Mary. That rocking, cradling instinct, I suspect, remains lifelong in mothers. "Jesus," it turned out that night, was an Asbury Seminary student. I had watched Jeff on our turf and had talked with him in my office when his hair was reaching full costume style. His presence everywhere in the weeks preceding the performance compelled me to watch him move that night from triumph to crucifixion and death with more than passivity or indifference.

Parents continue their bonding through automatic and insignificant gestures every day. The communication literally flows. By some communications estimates, your messages ride only about 5 percent on words and about 95 percent on facial contact, body language, and vocal tone and inflection. The same percents seem to hold true for all communication. Besides this, the early years see you having physical contact with the child. Mothers nurse the infant, both parents handle the child in bathing, bedtime, and frolicking playtime activities. Even discipline that may involve holding, restraining, or even spanking the child are bonding events. Indeed, even abusive parents who beat their children are amazed to find that the child embraces the violent parent. The psychological deformities may turn up later in a violent teen or young adult, but the solidarity of abusive families is a silent and terrifying witness to the power of personal bonding, even when it is abusive.

Parents log unbelievable hours of intimate voice, touch, and social contact with their children. The impressions left in the child's memory of verbal and nonverbal messages, the odors, the warmth of touch, the indescribably candid shots of parental behavior in every imaginable emotional state—together these form a gigantic bonding deposit.

If you are anything like us, you have recited bedtime stories until they are patented in your own version. We recently repeated "Wee Willie Winkie" in the special spooky version we had used with Heather when she was a toddler. Now at eleven, she still went through the same muscular contractions, displaying mild fear that we had triggered with the nighttime telling when she was three.

Parents leave their mark on the child, and it is little wonder that the bonds carry them through the reverse care years of old age when they become like children dependent on their own children. "But Mother, I'm supposed to be the little girl asking you what to wear," one of our friends found herself saying when her mother asked directions much as the daughter had done fifty years ago.

### Sibling Bonding

Since all of us are programmed to parent, the older brothers and sisters stand in line to care for the newborn. This parentlike care sets up bonds very much like the parent-infant bond. They are alike, too, when the bonds need to be severed to let the emerging adult go free.

When Justin was born, Heather and Lesli were permitted only to view him through the glass on the second floor of Central Baptist Hospital in Lexington. Lesli had heard Grandma Joy whisper into Heather's ear, as she held her up to see Justin, "There's your baby." So, when Lesli's turn came, she asked, "If Justin is Heather's baby, where's my baby?" She thought there would be enough to go around, what with a whole room full of them. Both girls have mothered him all these years.

The magic of sibling bonding, the bonding between children in a family, rides partly on the mysterious instinct by which even an infant can locate the youngest member of a clan in only a few seconds. Who can explain how an infant decides which person in the room is nearest to its perceptual world? They want to link up and be nurtured by that child.

## Place Bonding

Who can say how we become attached to home and to the locale of our origin or of our years of critical development? As a young high school boy I entered music competition at the local and district levels using a song entitled "The Hills of Home." It was obviously written by a person from a mountain environment. I have no idea where my teacher, Norma Wendelburg, found it or why she assigned it to me. I did my best and came home with a superior rating. I was a flatlander of the most extreme sort. Western Kansas is big sky country, and only my occasional visits to the Rocky Mountains three hundred miles away furnished me any images at all for singing the song. I could not then imagine living in the mountains.

What I was to learn within a few months was that after being away to college, there was an enormous tranquilizing effect waiting for me at home. I was glad to be grown up and away. On my first visit back for a holiday, I visited into the night with the family, fell in bed before midnight, and slept through two nights and one whole day. I still cannot believe it, but something in me let go and relaxed.

Across the years, I still find it true that I am able to come home emotionally when I get near the soil, the sun, and the stars of my boyhood. I have even speculated that it is because I literally lived on the soil, ate its food, and that I consumed the literal molecules formed from that soil, under that sun, and stars. During my first fifteen years, most of what I ate came from that soil. I concluded that bonding to place is a matter of the heart and the images of home and security.

I doubt that anyone has described a place bonding episode better than Robert Coles in a chapter he calls "A Domain of Sorts." He reports on some respected but anonymous families from Wolfe County, Kentucky, one of which is assigned the name of Kenneth Workman. They live, he says, in a cabin in what is called Deep Hollow.

"If we're going to be good parents," Kenneth told me,

we've got to teach our kids a lot about Deep Hollow, so they can find their way around and know everything they've got to know. It's their home, the hollow is. People who come here from outside are not likely to figure out that we've got a lot of teaching to do for our kids outside of school, and it's not the kind they'll get in books. My boy Danny has got to master the hollow; that's what my dad used to say to me; all the time he would tell me and tell me and then I'd be in good shape for the rest of my life.

How does Danny get to master the hollow? For one thing, he was born there, and his very survival augurs well for his future mastery. Laura received no medical care while she carried Danny; the boy was delivered by his two aunts, who also live is Deep Hollow. Danny's first encounter with the Appalachian land took place minutes after he was taken, breathing and screaming, from his mother. Laura describes what happened: "Well, as I can recall, my sister Dorothy came over and showed him to me, and then he was making so much noise we knew he was all right. His birthday is July tenth, you see, and it was a real nice day. She brought me a pail of blackberries that she'd picked and she said they were for later. When Danny was born Dorothy took him over and showed him the blackberries and said it won't be long before he'll be eating them, but first he'll have to learn to pick them, and that will be real soon. Then he was still crying, and she asked me if I didn't think he ought to go outside and see his daddy's corn growing up there, good and tall, and the chickens we have, and Spot and Tan, because they're going to be his dogs, just like everyone else's. I said, to go ahead, and my sister Anne held me up a little so I could see, and the next thing I knew the baby was out there near Ken's corn, crying as loud as he could.

Ken held him high over his head and point him around like he was one of the guns being aimed. I heard him telling the baby that here was the corn, there was the beets, and there was cucumbers, and here was the lettuce, and there was the best laying chicken we've got. Next thing he told the baby to stop the crying—and he did, he just did. Ken has a way with kids, even as soon as they're born. He told him to shush up, and he did, and then he just took him and put him down over there near the corn, and the other kids and my sisters all stood and looked. Dorothy was going to pick him up and bring him back to me, but Ken said he was fast asleep and quiet, and let him just lie there and we should all go and leave things be for a while. So they did; and Ken came in and told me I'd done real well, and he was glad to have a red-haired son, at last, what with two girls that have red hair but all the boys with brown hair. He said did I mind the little fellow lying out there near his daddy's farm getting to know Deep Hollow, and I said, no, why should I.[5]

I am older now, and I am in Kentucky. Now I can sing "The Hills of Home" with genuine feeling. Since 1977, I have taken backpacking adventures into those ancient sandstone and iron mountains of eastern Kentucky. I have literally walked from Morehead to Tennessee, virtually across the entire state.

The Red River Gorge is my second home. I sleep on the forest floor there for fourteen nights every summer. When I approach the Slade exit or drop west off I-75 toward Yahoo Falls further south, or slip off the Livingston exit northeast toward the civil war battleground accessible only by the Sheltowee Trace, I sense that this is my home. I understand God's promise to Abraham, "Wherever the soles of your feet touch the ground, I give that land to you."

We are created from the dust of the earth: Adam from *adama*. Our linkage to soil and place is not only psychological and grounded in experience, it seems also to be grounded in chemistry. So we will be sensitive to place in our emotional bonding galaxy.

*Pair Bonding*

My major thesis on pair bonding appears elsewhere. There, I trace the Creation concept of "two becoming one flesh" and Jesus' caution to protect the intimacy bond: "What therefore God joins together, let no one put asunder."[6]

The keystone of the entire bonding structure in the human family is the exclusive, lifelong bond that forms between a man and a woman. Community is everywhere written into the lifechain. Indeed, it appears as if the Judeo-Christian understanding of "Fall" as the tragic loss of the original intention for humanity is larger than our single species. Animals, birds, and reptiles seem also to be marked by varying degrees of exclusive monogamous pair bonding, with the larger proportion of them having to live out a defective bonding arrangement within their species.

The mystery of the intimacy bond sets up a condition, where it is healthy, in which the family experiences solidarity, mutual respect, and high fidelity. Indeed, we have seen in our examination of family systems that the intimate family predicts the most stable children as they are launched into a troubled social environment. In contrast, those households marked by conflict, deception, or domination tend to launch children who are deformed by the imperfect bond between the parents.

Adultery or promiscuity places an enormous stress on a marriage and a family. In *Re-Bonding*, I have defined these tragic patterns and their effects on intimate relationships. When I had done so at a great university in Los Angeles not long ago, one young man turned himself in afterward. "I cannot believe that you know me, yet you were describing me when you told how a promiscuous man carries himself and how he is helplessly caught in a pattern of sexual addiction. You said that I am 'hollow.' That is exactly my case. What is worse than anything is that I am right now dating a woman I would like to marry. She is a dream, but I cannot even be faithful to her while I am dating her. I'm promiscuous all the time."[7]

It turns out that the twelve steps of pair bonding are essential agendas for the entire lifetime of a relationship. Eye and voice contact, particularly, are eroded in many families today because of the theft of time and bonding energy that now goes into television viewing. Families that do not eat at the same table at the same time also miss out on essential bonding time.

### Intergenerational Bonding

Earlier in this book I told of Steve Seamands's powerful attachment to his grandfather, kept alive through a photograph of his infant baptismal ceremony. When Richard Heintzenreiter and I exchanged stories of our spiritual pilgrimage when we were guests at Emory University in 1984, he told a similar story of his attachment to his grandfather. He told how his grandparents were very committed Christians who attended a summer family conference each year. Dick looked forward to going with them each summer. It was in that setting that he was profoundly converted and began a personal walk with God.

Richard's story is much like my own. Grandparents tend to have a stronger leverage on their grandchildren than they did on their own children in matters of faith and values. Perhaps it is because their faith and values are more ripened and less brittle. Grandparents are less likely to come off in authoritarian ways—to know that major battles are won mostly by relationships and less often by verbal assaults.

The poetry of this intergenerational bonding turns out to be the genetic fluke that keeps baffling families everywhere. It boils down to this: your grandchildren are more likely to look like you than your own children are. Child abuse studies have found the phenomenon to be crucial in tracing the sources behind describing the scapegoat syndrome. Many times in an abusive family, the child is abused who reminds a parent of unfinished business with their own parent.

All that is needed for intergenerational bonding to occur is proximity and time. Most children today do not have access to grandparents, uncles, and aunts. If they are available, there is a magical magnet that attaches children to relatives. It is as if they accept immediately the possibility of modeling their lives on these important and accessible relatives.

Robert Coles found a boy he calls Billy Potter in Logan County, West Virginia, near Rocky Creek. At eight years of age, Billy already feels attached to his community and connected to his several generations:

> For me, this is the best place to be in the whole world. I've not been to other places, I know; but if you have the best place right round you, before your eyes, you don't have to go looking. . . .
>
> If I left here and went to live in a city, I'd be losing everything—that's what I hear said by my father and my uncle and cousins. We've been here so long, it's as long as when the country was started. My people came here and they followed the

creek up to here and they named it Rocky Creek; they were the ones, that's right. In the Bible we have written down the names of our kin that came before us and when they were born and when they died, and my name is there and I'm not going to leave here, because there'd be no mention of me when I get married and no mention of my children, if I left the creek.[8]

The power of the family clan is rarely so strong as this threat to leave our names out of the family Bible, but intergenerational bonding that enhances our identity search is badly needed by today's families.

## Deformed Bonding

In four earlier chapters we looked at family systems. In three of the four systems, it was clear that whatever bonding occurred would have been deformed. Review the bonding consequences laid down in classical family vignettes from the Bible:

*Competitive system.* Isaac and Rebecca split the loyalty of their sons Esau and Jacob, putting Esau at risk to marry into the fast lane where the wicked women were. Jacob, with the deceptive trickery and tutorial help of his mother Rebecca, managed to split the family over the inheritance. Exiled in search of a wife, he used deception and suffered from counterdeception until he was finally reconciled with Esau.

*Chaotic system.* The sons of Eli the high priest were disobedient and undisciplined. Perhaps this is a chaotic family. Devoted to his religious office, Eli was married to his vocation and lost his sons.

*Showcase system.* David, himself the youngest son of Jesse, was overlooked in the search for a king, simply because his family placement was not in superior rank, a sign of the power and authority model. He himself ran a similar family ship. He took the liberties that are so common to authority-hungry men: he arranged a sexual liaison with another man's wife. The intimacy was compounded by her husband's murder at the front lines of battle. The ricochet effect of his adultery circled through his family until rape, incest, and murder were quickly added. The fast lane of high visibility, or celebrity fame, tends very quickly to corrupt in the show-case species of troubles.

*Intimacy system.* Here there is no predictable deformity in family bonding. Take a look at the holy family. Joseph, Mary, and Jesus are linked ahead of their time to Creation and beyond their time to the vision of full redemption. Joseph was bonded to Jesus through a birthing experience that defied local or prevailing custom anywhere in the world. The two of them launched Jesus into adult responsibility essentially at age twelve, and when Jesus missed the caravan leaving Jerusalem, Mary was able to speak the words of interrogation. All of them negotiated a way to show absolute respect for each other as the solution to a wasted three days lost in searching for the lost boy. Ideal bonding is no guarantee that there will not be tense or painful moments, but it is a way of predicting that pain and loss will be processed in constructive and not destructive ways.

In this chapter, I have wanted you to see the many faces of intimacy and to trace the powerful forces that attach us to each other. In our privatized world, it is easy to assume that each of us can fix whatever goes wrong, and we can do it by ourselves. What is more probable is that we are all linked together in multiple networks, and that we are sustained or damaged by those relationships. The rather long list of bonding possibilities I have outlined here is only a beginning. I have eliminated nearly half of the possibilities I could identify. So write your own list of good resources available to you as you seek to risk proof your household through generating strong patterns of family and community life.

## QUESTIONS PEOPLE ASK

*Q: You make it sound like bonding is a new discovery. What did we call it before the word was coined?*

A: I first saw the pair-bonding language about ten years ago, though it was likely in use before that time to refer specifically to the mysterious attachment we experience in parent-child and in adult-sexual relationships, as well as in occasional friendship contexts. In the 1930s there were studies of imprinting, and if you read some of them you will see that what they observed and described could easily be called bonding. It is important to remember that words are symbols. They merely represent reality and are not reality itself. So in any living language new words have to be invented to describe new or expanding perceptions of reality—as is the case with the word "bonding." At the same time any living language is abandoning words that cease to describe the reality they first gestured toward. When a language becomes a dead language, such as Latin is today, it means that the language is no longer expanding to match newer perceptions of reality, so is no longer changing, hence is dead.

*Q: What a surprise to see you talking about place bonding, yet it rings true for me. My parents moved to Texas from Florida when I was only six years old. My younger brother and sister seem to have no memory of Florida, but when I returned last summer to the community where I grew up, I had a strange sense that I was home. That was amazing.*

A: It is not surprising when we consider that human bonding rides on touch, sight, sound, and taste, plus other more profound sensations we still do not have simple names to describe. When we live in an environment it is imprinted on our memory by those sensations. I was astonished to think about how I became accustomed to sounds until they actually bond to security for me. While living near Winona Lake, we were only a quarter mile from the Pennsylvania Railroad with its high speed passenger service and its endless freight trains. For the first two weeks in our new home we were awake through the night with every train, but then we programmed the sound into our expectations. Our overnight guests, however, would comment at breakfast about the punctuation of trains through the night. Similarly, our sons, early in childhood before we had air conditioning, grew accustomed to the muffled roar of an oscillating fan while they slept. To this day, these adult men prefer to sleep in a room with a light motor noise—a case of sound bonding. So place bonding is easy to recognize because of the various sensation levels at which we become attached.

# 13

# *Family Systems,*
# *Children, and Faith*

△

We met the Matsons when their oldest son was entering high school. The children were alternate brother, sister, brother, sister, and were scattered over about eight years. Eventually we saw them all through the youth ministry program where we had about four hours of contact with the group each week.

Anyone who works with junior high or senior high people knows that if you get the luxury of working with siblings during their teen years, you will be enthralled with the differences you see within the same family. I now have handles for describing the differences, but in those days I could only celebrate them, and the Matson kids were wildly diverse in their approaches to life and in the way they worked with other people.

Del and Dean, the brothers were both very introverted. I would have called them quiet or reserved. Both were gifted in many ways and couldn't escape leadership roles among their peers, although they didn't seem to be seeking to lead. One night Dean responded to an open prayer altar, and afterward I offered a few supportive statements, but it was clear that he neither needed nor intended to let anyone know what he had given over to God.

The daughters were as extroverted as any with whom we have worked. Once or twice I had no alternative but to listen to schemes and plots that curdled my blood. "Let's play off two or three scenarios," I suggested one evening when Ann and her friend Betsy had stopped by my office to ventilate some wrath. When I had offered the possible outcomes, they seemed more calm and didn't carry out their most recent threat.

What I am describing for you is a family of children that, while very different in approaching all of life, have one thing in common. Now, thirty years later, all four of them are launching families of their own and all are profoundly rooted in deep and active faith.

Once when Dean apologized for missing an early morning support group with whom I met, I responded, "Dean, I don't think you need the group as much as some of those teens do. You have resources in your family that many of them don't have." My instincts, untutored by wide empirical studies, were very close to the truth.

John Westerhoff raises the question *Will Our Children Have Faith?* Walter Bruggeman has answered him with another question: "Will Our Faith Have Children?"[1]

I noted long ago that God has no grandchildren, by which I intended to suggest that parents cannot pass the torch of faith to children in any sort of secondhand way, but that children must come to experience God personally in each generation.[2]

Today I would likely phrase the issue in other terms. It is clear that parents have the power to create environments that predict the transfer of faith and values. It is equally clear that they cannot guarantee that faith will ignite in their children.

So in this final chapter, I want to explore the interface between family systems and the issue of how to predict faith issues with children.

## Roots of Faith

Every human being seems to arrive on this planet equipped and motivated to do faith.[3] The direction in which faith is focused is by no means fixed, and the objects of adoration occupy the full spectrum from evil to good. People who claim to have no faith, for example, are lying. They are simply unaware of the focus of their faith energy. This universal endowment and inclination to have faith in external sources of authority, control, or help is adequately described, perhaps, by the concept that God has gifted all humans with the image of God. This inner capacity to be in touch with external resources thus equips every person to reach out and to bestow the honor of dependency on some external perceived reality. It is beside the point whether that reality is science, money, success, demonic evil, or the God of all truth and righteousness: all humans are faithing beings. We simply cannot point to any other species and identify behaviors that seem to be characterized by such a persistent devotion to external faith images. Those who wish to have a tangible, empirical proof of faith may remain unconvinced. Michelangelo cut open a cadaver in the dead house of a monastery in the full expectation of finding the soul somewhere in the thoracic cavity. More modern attempts have been made to link the spiritual core of human existence with some tangible, material substance. The most profound realities of love and hate are not empirically quantifiable, although the evidences of them can be observed, filmed, and studied through the behaviors each evokes. Perhaps it is enough that we use the same tools for studying the faith behavior of humans. We can document people in acts of faith expression, and we can interrogate them about why they do such things. Such a procedure leaves us firmly grounded in social science research.

### Core Content of Faith

Laying aside religious and theological definitions, it is clear that two motors drive the faith dimension of all humans. One of these is described in research as a sense of attachment.[4] Attachment means the universal human inclination to reach out and to establish significant connections with other humans. The other is best described as a core of justice.[5] The justice impulse seems to be constantly monitoring events and especially human transactions looking for the impact among persons and judging them in terms of fairness, equality, or equity. The first impulse to attach accounts for the entire sphere of human friendship and love. The second impulse for justice accounts for much of human energy devoted to the regulation of interpersonal, social, even international relationships.

So when anyone speaks of a search for meaning or for significant relationships, we are likely listening to the deepest human soundings at the core of the faith appetite. Not all faith systems—for example, money, power, success—can satisfy the core needs we feel. It is important that we acknowledge the universality of the faithing appetite.

Throughout this book I have been asking you to consider two major features of relationships in the family system. These measure the positive or negative directions on the axis of value of persons and the high or low distribution of responsibility. It is not by accident that the first measures an issue at the core of attachment or love concerns, and the second gives us a profile on the justice issue. When we see attachment as love and justice as righteousness and integrity, we see that we are looking into the face of the core of Judeo-Christian faith. It would be too simple to suggest that all faithful adherents in those two faith communities score high on value of persons and high on distribution of responsibility. It would be valid to suggest that people saturated in those faith traditions might be expected to see the importance of scoring highest on both scales.[6]

## Family Systems and Faith

Here we come to the central issue of this book. Since the family and its total combination of exchanges and agendas is the matrix in which the child is formed, the roots and content of faith are powerfully shaped by what happens in the family. This means that a child's views of God, of love, of justice, of sin, of forgiveness, and of goodness or righteousness are powerfully shaped by the experiences in the family. I spoke in chapter 2 of the first curriculum. That curriculum is not in books, but in people, in interpersonal transactions. To say it theologically, parents are the image of God to their children.

That may seem to be a heavy load, suggesting that parents are being asked to do something for God which they never agreed to do: to teach about God. Think of it another way: God has agreed to live with whatever image you project of who He is. So it turns out that parents are given full freedom and authority to form their child's perceptions about the core issues on which faith will emerge. Put at its very lowest and most frightening level, the Creator has distributed responsibility to every human pair as if to say: "You are God to this child. You created the child. You will also provide the data that fills the God-shaped vacuum in the child. That faith motor will take on the characteristics of the two of you. You are creating images on which a whole life of faith will be constructed."

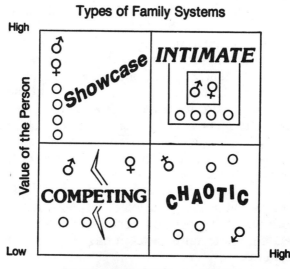

If you complain that you are not ready for such responsibility, check the four-quadrant chart again. God has distributed responsibility to the highest possible degree. He has done so because of the highest possible value He places on every person. God trusts you with your fertility. God trusts every couple with their sexual energy. God hinges every generation on the persistent and unconditional care that parents give their children. So if you think the model of the intimate family has too many risks in it, remember that God has been taking that risk from the moment of the human creation and continues to do so.

Before we look at the predictable faith building blocks that emerge from each of the four quadrant systems, look at some basic projections from the two axes.

## Faith and the Value of Persons

People who have a high regard for the value of other people consistently have a high value of self. To love God with all your heart and your neighbor as yourself suggests that the love level will be either consistently high with regard to God, others, and self, or consistently low.

Many faith systems move on a low view of the value of persons. This is especially true of the money, sex, and power gods that consistently regard all persons as objects. What is not so clear is that the charlatans who wield the sword in those adventures also have a low view of themselves. Suicide adventures into money, sex, and power must not be confused with heroic self-sacrifice in behalf of the safety and welfare of others. More orthodox faith systems also move on a low view of persons. Systems that stress the badness of people, their intrinsic untrustworthiness and proneness to deceit and sinfulness of everybody turn a lot of us loose with deformed ideas both about people and about God. You can see how deformed our basic faith perceptions can be as a result of family systems:

In the eyes of people who have a consistently low view of persons, *God* is a tyrant whose principal business is punishing wrongdoers and harassing them; *love* means manipulating people to get what you want; *justice* is using violence to punish those who hurt you, and it is knowing that if you get caught, all hell will break loose.

If a high view of persons dominates, God is seen as benevolent and all knowing, but approachable and quickly forgiving.

Love is known as unconditional and noncoercive or manipulable. Justice is knowing that everything comes out fairly and that consequences are appropriate to the choice, not punitive or deadly.

## Faith and the Distribution of Responsibility

A most amazing spectrum of faith appears along the axis that measures distribution of responsibility, authority, and power. Who would think that a family system paints images of God, of love, and of justice in the minds of people within those systems?

When a low distribution of responsibility characterizes the family relationships we see one person dominating the lives of all others. Look at some of the life habits and perceptions that are predictable: *God* is totally responsible for everything—to be the magician, the monarch, the provider, without any response at all from persons who see themselves as powerless children. They find themselves most often in the helpless, beggar role. When they pray they spend most of their time asking for things they want—much as children making a Christmas list. If they do not get what they want, God may be seen as a tyrant, a whimsical and incompetent deity. They then tend to rebel, to resist God much as they may have resisted a tyrannical parent.

*Righteousness* is seen as exclusively the responsibility of God and sometimes as an accusation placed against other people. There is a tendency to criticize all authority figures, expecting perfection from them but an unwillingness to lift a hand to be personally responsible or to clean up that person's own life or attitudes.

In contrast to the low end of the responsibility axis, people who experience early and consistent high responsibility in the family tend to see themselves as workers with God, as having dominion, and being responsible for what happens, even though other persons are the principal actors. They sense that they can make a difference, that God has allowed them to be participants in daily and even global events and issues that shape the future. Edmund Burke's famous statement is clearly from a high responsibility perspective:

I am one.
I am only one.
I cannot do everything.
But I can do something.
What I can do I will do.
I am one.
But I am one.

If there has been serious violation of the person, we are likely to see an icy cold autonomy develop in which the self-made person emerges with a heartless attitude toward other people and toward God, declaring that it is everyone for themselves. Ironically this personality may have been in mind when Jesus said, "Those who are whole do not need a physician." Ministry and help are more often accepted by people who have been bruised in the responsibility struggle than by those who have successfully carved out their own turf and have achieved the goals they set for themselves. Those who have been victims of injustice tend to polarize. They either become compassionate champions of the oppressed or cold egomaniacs out to settle their own damages for the rest of their lives.

It may be helpful to look at the four quadrants of the family systems grid and to predict some basic faith dimensions that tend to appear in those systems.

### Faith in the Competitive System

*God.* Here in this low-low corner of the two dimensions we are examining, God is seen as the great magician in the sky who responds to making deals. Typical prayer involves a lot of begging and not a little bargaining for proofs of God's favor and that the one who is asking is a good boy or a good girl. Since there is very little spontaneous communication in the competitive family system, prayer rarely focuses upon communion, praise, thanksgiving, or celebration. Instead, prayer is self-centered and manipulative, just as most transactions in the family tend to be. Regularized church attendance and religious rituals of private devotions or Bible reading tend to be efforts to win points on which the person can collect from God when trouble comes. Prayer is paying dues to the super-parent God in order to have a bargaining position with Him.

*Sin.* The worst thing that can happen in the competitive system is to be caught playing up to the other parent and making deals there. It is not surprising to see a concept of sin emerge in this competitive family that sees humiliation, embarrassment, and getting caught as essentially the worst thing that can happen. Since these are egocentric feelings and are rooted in shame, there can be no repentance, only an attempt to reestablish an image of being in step again with the super-parent. Shame and this view of sin is essentially narcissistic and never leads to spiritual wholeness or to advancing in maturity; the shame-based sinner remains forever a child playing childish games. If people grow up and see through this childish game of religious shame, it is common for them to repudiate religion all together and move ahead as straightforward and honest secular egomaniacs.

*Love.* Competitive systems relationships tend to deform love and to freeze it into self-seeking and self-gratifying modes. Since it is locked into a low view of persons, it tends to be arrested at a low level of trust. Suspicion and jealousy are common among these family members. Since deception and theft are common in such a system, friendships and even marriages tend to suspect the worst, to be overly possessive and demanding in the relationship.

*Justice.* Fairness is the preoccupation of the competitive system. Since fairness is always focused on the self and on protecting the rights and the viewpoint of the self, there is a heavy use of justice language, but always in self-defense or self-advancement. The alternate heartbeat of righteousness tends to show up in concepts of positional righteousness, without serious awareness of the idea of being made righteous or thoroughly holy. Even salvation is seen most often as a mere covering or cloak instead of a real change of character or of life substance. This superficial view of how God's grace works is convenient to the egocentric person who wishes the appearance of faith without paying the price of allowing grace to transform the core of life and of values.

*Faith in the Chaotic Family*

*God.* Here the unpredictable household leaves the persons with a view of God as inconsistent, distant, and unreliable. The self-made member of this family may find outside reliable models and come to faith with a perspective based on that mentor, surrogate parent, pastor, or neighbor. Agnosticism is rampant in the circle of members in chaotic families. This agnosticism links up with the typical pattern of undisciplined personal life, so the low self-esteem person is easily seduced into a further hole: God does not exist and there is no meaning in life. Unlike the self-made family member, remaining members of the chaotic family tend to suffer from disintegration of personality. Lack of regularity, order, discipline, and consistent affection frequently leave them at risk to stress, personality disorders, and needing psychiatric or mental patient care. Since parents were not dependable sources of care and guidance, they have difficulty in seeing God as the source of all comfort, yet they need more help than most people to find that resource available to them.

*Sin.* There is little awareness of sin in chaotic families. They are nicely described in 1 John 1:10: "If we claim we have not sinned, we make him out to be a liar and his word has no place in our lives." The complete vacuum of God's word in the form of God's first curriculum, namely, parental care, leaves them with a vague form of malaise and depression. Unfortunately, they have no language or conception by which to describe their generalized black mood as sin. Within the chaotic family the natural consequences of human failure make their mark. Since there are no parents to supervise or intervene, they find that messing up and having to deal with the consequences comes at a high price. Often in their self-centeredness and narcissism they simply sweep the issues under the rug, deny responsibility, or run away from their own trouble. Alienation and long-term dishonesty in relationships is a common pattern. If they are trapped and cannot run away, the pain of dealing with consequences sometimes makes them more careful not to go against the grain of moral responsibility and a measure of moral maturity seems to appear. In the chaotic family there is little confession or forgiveness, and even when caught, it is common that the family members ostracize the offending person to teach them a lesson. Relentless scapegoating is common in chaotic families, primarily because parental referees do not balance out the accusations and level the responsibilities among the children, but also because one way for all people, including parents, to cover their feelings of guilt for neglecting the family is to blame somebody, and a child is as good a scapegoat as anyone else.

*Love.* As with the competitive system, love tends to be extremely self-centered, controlling, manipulative, and self-serving. Unlike the competitive family system, however, the chaotic structure serves notice on the child that anything they want will have to be searched out by themselves. The passivity of the competitive system child tends to be traded here for a much more active searching for love, still on its own terms, still jealous, punitive, and exploitive. The child immobilized by the chaotic system's lack of order and discipline may be unable to reach out for relationships, so the disintegration of personality is complicated by the isolation created when every other family member flies off in separate directions, leaving the lonely and immobilized member without social contact of any kind.

*Justice.* The self-protection essential in a chaotic family again defines the justice and righteousness issues much like those described above for the competitive family system. Whereas the child of the competitive family finds justice violations and settlements primarily in the household relationships, the chaotic family member has to engage the whole world. Fairness becomes an issue with people met on the street, at school, or any other public arena. Chaotic family members are somewhat more likely to be involved in fights, arguments, and protection of turf than are members of any other system. In the vacuum created by abdicated responsibility for the safety and welfare of the family, the child is an easy nominee for gang leader or for a more passive follower of a cult leader who leads with charisma and promises reward. Any appeal to self-interest tends to win the support of the more passive member of the chaotic family. Following the massacre at Jonestown, Guiana, it was startling to all of us to discover that literally hundreds of the victims had no identifiable relatives to claim the bodies. These were clearly cult-dependent followers who were spawned in chaotic family systems.

## Faith in the Showcase Family

*God.* In this highly vertical power structure, God is the superparent modeled on the family member who wields the power. That image of God will imprint into the minds of all family members, not simply the children. So God is imaged typically in authoritarian, autocratic, even punitive ways. If the power base parent is benevolent, generous, and forgiving, of course God will be pictured in the same way. In any event, the human is consistently passive, the recipient of grace or of judgment, and sees answers to prayer as wonderful magic and unanswered prayer as likely God's way of punishing because of past personal failure. It is ironic that even though this quadrant highlights a high value of the person, the autocratic parent throws the family into a low theological self-esteem and into passivity simply by usurping all responsibility in the authoritarian grasp for control. This omniscient parent role eclipses prayer, for example, until it is reduced to begging or appealing, as if to the omniscient benefactor in the sky. The patterns are much like those in the low-value-of-person quadrants simply because of the power squeeze. Here we have a power hunger cultivated and a struggle to reach the rite of passage, usually marriage, when the power is transferred and the authoritarian payoff makes two decades of passive acceptance tolerable. "Wait until I have my own wife and family, and I will tell them what to do" is a common pacifier to a young man coming up in the chain-of-command family. It is not uncommon for personal commitment to faith to be frustrated until that authority is grasped and the weight of it confirms to the young husband and father that he must indeed turn to God now for the umbrella of protection he deserves as the authority center in the home. For women in the showcase family system, the move toward personal faith is typically stymied. She is likely locked into an inferior and childlike position and may not reach mature faith unless she is able to serve as a catalyst to transform the marriage and the family into the intimate system where responsibility is distributed and women and children are released to come to the full stature of their possibilities in faith.[7]

*Sin.* No family system evokes more of a sense of sin than the showcase family. Whatever emotions of self-centered shame may appear, the power center in the showcase system broadcasts regular and powerful messages about what is expected. So guilt is quickly put in place: failure to meet the demands of external authority jerks the culprit into line and sends shockwaves of guilt through the person. While this sense of sin is of a higher order and has more growth possibilities than that of either the competitive or the chaotic system, there is a tendency for guilt to become pathological here because it is tied primarily to external authority and the stress is on good appearances. So being good or feeling guilty for failure tend to be locked into pleasing other people and often especially behaving so things look right even when they are not. Since being good is primarily a matter of obeying the rules handed down from the authority source above, rule-keeping as an end in itself frequently becomes more important than being a person of integrity and of honesty based in substantive character and thoughtful positioning on a moral or prudential issue. Children from showcase families tend to have to sow their wild oats, since their conscience has remained external—in the parents—much too long. Since full authority and responsibility lie with the powerful parent, a defective or at least empty conscience tends to emerge, and there is frequently a spin-out phase that lasts from one to ten years before the value core is internalized as an autonomous adult.

*Love.* Relationships in the showcase family are almost entirely vertical. There are no peers. One spouse is over or beneath the other spouse. Child is over child either because of birth order or gender. Clear patterns, chains of command, appear even when undefined or unspoken. So the concept of developing relationships inevitably takes on vertical dimensions. Males typically assume that they initiate relationships and are often baffled if the female opens the door to friendship. Females are likely to take the passive stance and are hardly distinguishable from the low-esteem passive children of the competitive or chaotic family. Male-to-male friend-ships tend to move on the macho track of exclusive activities related to sports, work, or hunting and fishing. Female-to-female relationships tend, because of this verticalization pat-tern, also to be constructed around clubs, study groups, the kitchen, and sex-appropriate stereotypic activities. So long as they keep within their proper rank these relationships tend to have high loyalty and warmth. These, after all, are high-value-of-person relationships, and so long as the relationships can conform to the vertical chain-of-command roles, they are comfortable. When these people appear in larger groups, they tend to grasp for power or to become even more passive than in two-person or small-group relationships. "Did some-body elect you president?" is a common, if unspoken, ques-tion that comes to mind when a showcase kid climbs the emerging chain of command and takes over. Unlike the com-petitive system child who tends to undermine community by criticizing and conspiring to upset plans of the group, or the lone ranger, chaotic-system child who cannot relate to anyone intimately and well, the showcase child wants to verticalize everything in sight and to work the way to the top. "Vote on everything," this kid demands. "Campaign, make speeches, and debate" is the cry of persons who want to grasp con-trolling power. Their view of structure is so indelible that they assume everybody else agrees and cannot imagine why their organizing speech was interpreted as running for presi-dent. More often than not, people produced by competing and chaotic systems are so nonplused by the assertive confi-dence of the showcase kid that they themselves campaign for electing the aspiring power-hungry leader. When this hap-pens, a symbiotic set of relationships is often set in motion that can sustain itself over the long term, during which time the powerful acquire more power and the electorate forfeits more and more responsibility, quite willingly and gladly turning it over to the "professional." Whether in a political dictatorship or in a showcase family, the forfeiture of respon-sibility leaves the weak powerless and tends to push the pow-erful to tyrannical isolation.

*Justice.* What is fair and right is what the rules say when you hear it from people in the showcase family. The rules, of course, consist both of written and unwritten codes and laws. They cannot distinguish between rules and principles, although they often use the word principles to add weight to their rule systems. A principle contains no specific and concrete words to which adherence is required, but it sets limits based on values and relationships. Jesus's command: "Love your neighbor as you love yourself" is a principle, but it could not be adjudicated by a court of law because there are no specific behavioral measurements for it. Moses' "Thou shalt not kill" is a law, and a court or jury would have little trouble looking for evidence of death and murder. So justice or righteousness for the showcase family consists simply of strict adherence to rules and laws already set down. "I did exactly what I was supposed to do" excuses any violence that may have occurred. If there is the slightest ambiguity about what was supposed to be done, the showcase family member will insist on further clarification. There ought to be a law. Laws and rules proliferate wherever these people exert influence. You can see that this orientation to strict adherence to rules sets up the showcase family person to be vulnerable to a legal view of what constitutes goodness, righteousness, and justice. To the degree that goodness is seen in legalistic categories, we will not expect inner growth or sensitivity to issues of truth and righteousness or holiness to be significantly at work.

## Faith in the Intimate Family

*God.* Here in the high-value-of-persons and high-distribution-of-responsibility corner of our grid we will find parents whose image of God is one that stresses immanence, community, and partnership. Where father and mother are one and both discipline and affection are consistent and focused on future growth and responsibility, the view of God is that of a loving, just, and liberating parent who wants everyone to come to freedom, responsibility, and maturity in good time. Parents and children have access to each other. Celebration and conflict alike keep them in touch. There are no pockets of isolation or banishment from the community of the family. They have no problems but what we can solve together. Moving out as adults from such a family, there is a high sense that God is in partnership with them, that God has granted dominion and trusts them, and that they can trust other people. Prayer in the intimate system is largely focused on thanksgiving, celebration, and communion. Problems and high moments of victory are laid out before God, since God is near and is closely linked to everything important to them. They pray less for their own needs than any of the other systems groups, but they are often more sensitive to people and needs beyond their reach. Since they are not consumed in a search for power or for control, they have energy to reach far beyond their immediate world. Since they work with a full sense of the value of themselves, they assume that all other persons have value equal to theirs. Because of this, they are frequently ready to volunteer for emergency work or for life vocations that pour out energy in behalf of those for whom Christ died or simply out of compassion for suffering and disenfranchised people whose needs they have discovered.

*Sin.* Within the intimate system, sin most often consists of anything that damages relationships or desensitizes a sense of the value of persons or of the distribution of responsibility. These two factors converge to spotlight the highest values, and anything that violates either brings a sense of grief. These folks may speak of sin and of guilt, but they are more struck with a sense of loss, of forfeiture, of waste of nonreplaceable resources, or of the mangling of relationships. They perceive that a thing of beauty, of great potential, is now a ruin, but they also look toward restoration.

*Love.* Intimate system people, having such a high view of persons and such a wide latitude of shared responsibility, are ready to enter into respect-based relationships easily and are guided by concerns for the value of the persons themselves. They have no tolerance at all for relationships that use or exploit anyone. They have no interest in domineering roles within relationships. They have such a positive view of human creativity and gifts that they are likely to regard each relationship as one in which the roles are defined on the basis of the gifts that each brings to the relationship. This makes them remarkably free from concern about position, status, or roles in the workplace, in friendships, and in marriage and family issues. They are confident enough about their own worth, that they come to any situation or task knowing that whatever needs to be done, there will be gifted people available who can do it.

*Justice.* Concern in intimate systems families is for the protection of the rights and worth of all of the participants, indeed for people far beyond the family itself. They are concerned about foundational principles that express the respect for persons and the distribution of responsibility which grants freedom with dignity. They are able, more than any other group, to get beyond preoccupation with rules, laws, and reciprocal agreements in which everybody is treated the same. They are able to look after the interests of people who cannot claim equality and people who get overlooked by the system. When they speak of equity, the people from other systems rarely comprehend the concerns for adjusting justice to compensate people who have been handicapped by age, environment, or longstanding abuse so as to set them on their way with an advantage that begins to put them on a fair and equal footing with people with more fortunate roots.

### Toward Offering Faith to Our Children

What emerges as we look at family systems research is that faith is indeed caught from the total life of the family. When ancient Israel memorized the *Shema,* they were reminding themselves of their continuous instruction in the family: "Hear, O Israel: The Lord our God, the Lord is one. Love the Lord your God with all your heart and with all your soul and with all your strength. These commandments that I give you today are to be upon your hearts. Impress them on your children. Talk about them when you sit at home and when you walk along the road, when you lie down and when you get up. Tie them as symbols on your hands and bind them on your foreheads. Write them on the doorframes of your houses and on your gates" (Deut. 6:4-9).

Can you imagine an instruction more clear: *Be careful twenty-four hours each day, because you will be representing my character to your children.* Here the major focus is on parents and the child is the learner. Listen to Jesus make another point: "At that time the disciples came to Jesus and asked, 'Who is the greatest in the kingdom of heaven?' He called a little child and had him stand among them. And he said: 'I tell you the truth, unless you change and become like little children, you will never enter the kingdom of heaven. Therefore, whoever humbles himself like this child is the greatest in the kingdom of heaven. And whoever welcomes a little child like this in my name welcomes me. But if anyone causes one of these little ones who believe in me to sin, it would be better for him to have a large millstone hung around his neck and to be drowned in the depths of the sea'" (Matt. 18:1-6). Then little children were brought to Jesus for him to place his hands on them and pray for them. The disciples rebuked those who brought them.

Jesus said, "'Let the little children come to me, and do not hinder them, for the kingdom of heaven belongs to such as these.' When he had placed his hands on them, he went on from there" (Matt. 19:14-15).

If perpetual parenting not only bonds parent to child through daily talk, walk, and recitation of God's reality, but also bonds the child to the community of faith, then Jesus suggests that there remains another witness. God is resident in the young child and speaks to us. Whatever it was that Jesus saw in children, he labeled it belief and indicated that the kingdom of heaven belongs to such as these. So to be mature is somehow to become childlike, perhaps in trust, good will, and optimism. So the child calls us to faith, simply by its helplessness and its dependency upon us.

In this chapter I have wanted you to examine the four models of the family that emerge from family systems research. I most wanted you to see the enormous faith messages that are indelibly stenciled into the members of the family by the experiences in family relationships. It is clear that the intimate family is able to construct images and visions of God, of sin, of love, and of justice that more nearly represent God than any of the other families.

So in this book I offer you the best and most hopeful blueprint I know of by which to evaluate your present family system. Here, I think, you will have found some goals and some yardsticks by which to measure your success in adapting your family's relationships to those highest priorities: high value of persons and highest distribution of responsibility. I salute you in your pilgrimage in family, and continue my own trek sandwiched in the number-two slot in a four generation tribe.

## QUESTIONS PEOPLE ASK

*Q: If faith is a supernatural gift of God, how could the family system have anything to do with it?*
A: I am impressed by the fact that faith is not something that we do, but it is, like grace, God's gift. The gift is first an investment God makes in the Creation, so that all persons are born with what we could crudely call instinctual faith. That is, you cannot be human and not have an inclination toward trust in an outside source or adoration of an outside idol or God. So in some sense faith in embryo is a universal gift of God to humans. In the Judeo-Christian understanding of God's way of working, the image of God is invested in humans, and those humans then telegraph God's character, simply by being human. Then, in a special way, God breaks through to each of us in a direct faith encounter as we are called to surrender life and eternity to Jesus and to live in obedience to him. It is here that the family will have programmed us to hear that call in ways that have been shaped by our family experience. So we can predict that the people with the best preparation to see God for who He is are those who have had the intimate system as the first curriculum.

*Q: I am surprised that you did not offer a program for developing faith in the family by using regular Bible reading and prayer times. Did you overlook something important?*
A: I would like to put together a book of resources for families in their worship of God and their celebration of faith. I suspect that the most powerful curriculum in the home

consists of basic interpersonal relationships, how people treat each other, and how they show consistency and fairness day after day. I celebrate table graces and family prayers. I am even now collecting some of the most constructive models with a view to sharing them in another format. It is easy, however, to come to trust in routine and ritual, and family systems suggests that it is the quality of the environment that speaks most for God, not the forms or the litanies that might be used.

# Notes

△

Because this book is part of a series on bonding relationships, I have cited frequently the other books in the series. These books are as follows:

Donald M. Joy, *Bonding: Relationships in the Image of God* (Waco, Tex.: Word, 1985); hereafter referred to as *Bonding*.

————, *Re-Bonding: Preventing and Restoring Damaged Relationships* (Waco, Tex.: Word, 1986); hereafter referred to as *Re-Bonding*.

———— and Robbie B. Joy, *Lovers—Whatever Happened to Eden?* (Waco, Tex.: Word, 1987); hereafter referred to as *Lovers*.

### Chapter 2

1. For an expanded discussion of "encompassing mothers" and "engrossing fathers," see *Bonding*, esp. chap. 7, "Parents and Children: For Each Other." See also the chapters dealing with differences between "head" and "body" metaphors describing what women and men contribute to the whole-body concept in *Lovers*.

2. For extensive documentation on mothers' and fathers' responses to newborns, see M. H. Klaus and J. H. Kennell, *Parent-Infant Bonding*, 2d ed. (St. Louis: C. V. Mosby Co., 1976).

### Chapter 3

1. Ronald L. Koteskey attributes the coining of the term "invention of adolescence" to historian John Demos of Brandeis University and Virginia Demos of Harvard University. See their "Adolescence in Historical Perspective," *Journal of Marriage and the Family* 31 (1969): 632.

2. Ronald L. Koteskey, *Understanding Adolescence* (Wheaton, Ill.: Victor Books, 1987). Ron gives me credit for opening the question of a secular trend in the invention of adolescence. I was a guest speaker in his Sunday school class in the Wilmore (Ky.) United Methodist Church in 1976, long before the Koteskey children were adolescents. See page 37 for that drawing. The whole issue exploded, due in part to Ron's energy over the next several years. Over brown-bag lunches we encouraged each other in our efforts to publish. Eventually he took a position moderately different from mine in an article entitled "Adolescence: Unfortunate Creation of Western Society" that was accepted by *Christianity Today.* As we discussed his then-accepted article, I inquired whether he would mind if I offered the editors a "dialogic" article with an alternative evaluation of adolescence. He agreed with my idea of putting our somewhat contrasting evaluations side by side. I titled my article "Adolescence: Crucible for Creating Saints." They appeared as companion, not contrasting, articles in the 13 March 1981 issue, but the editors blunted both articles, calling his article "Growing Up Too Late, Too Soon." My article appeared as "Premature Puberty: Advice to Parents," and both articles were severely condensed to the point of almost losing the force of the issue.

3. See the entire article, including my stylized drawing showing the intersection of lines which "invent" adolescence in modern societies, in Roy B. Zuck and Warren S. Benson, *Youth Education in the Church,* 2d ed. (Chicago: Moody Press, 1978).

4. Here is the *New International Version* (NIV) of Luke 2:41–52, for your perusal in this discussion about "instant responsibility" at age twelve:

Every year his parents went to Jerusalem for the Feast of the Passover. When he was twelve years old, they went up to the Feast, according to the custom. After the Feast was over, while his parents were returning home, the boy Jesus stayed behind in Jerusalem, but they were unaware of it. Thinking he was in their company, they traveled on for a day. They began looking for him among their relatives and friends. When they did not find him, they went back to Jerusalem to look for him. After three days they found him in the temple courts, sitting among the teachers, listening to them and asking them questions. Everyone who heard him was amazed at his understanding and his answers. When his parents saw him, they were astonished. His mother said to him, "Son, why have you treated us like this? Your father and I have been anxiously searching for you."

"Why were you searching for me?" he asked. "Didn't you know I had to be in my Father's house?" But they did not understand what he was saying to them.

Then he went down to Nazareth with them and was obedient to them. But his mother treasured all these things in her heart. And Jesus grew in wisdom and stature, and in favor with God and men.

5. The diagram here was published in "Growing Up Too Late, Too Soon," *Christianity Today*, 13 March 1981, 26ff. It appears here by permission of the author.

6. This published version of my long-used transparency appeared in Zuck and Benson, *Youth Education in the Church*, 92.

7. See my treatment of potential causes of the secular trend in *Bonding*, 149–73.

8. Koteskey, *Understanding Adolescence*, 12–13, see esp. chap. 1.

9. If you wish to explore the connection between sexual development and the gift of bonding that occurs inevitably when a social relationship moves to sexual intimacy, see *Bonding* and *Re-Bonding*.

10. Gale D. Webbe, *The Night and Nothing* (New York: Seabury Press, 1964), 109, quoted in M. Scott Peck, *People of the Lie* (New York: Simon & Schuster, 1983), 269.

11. Peck, *People of the Lie*, 269.

12. C. S. Lewis, *The Lion, the Witch, and the Wardrobe* (New York: Collier/Macmillan, 1970), 160.

13. Peck, *People of the Lie*, 269.

### Chapter 4

1. B. F. Skinner, *Beyond Freedom and Dignity* (New York: Alfred A. Knopf, 1971). We are indebted to Skinner for taking his behaviorist theory to its logical conclusion, i.e., since each of us is shaped by forces outside ourselves, none of us is responsible for our existence or our behavior—thus, none of us is free to choose since what we think are free choices are simply the leverages of other forces outside ourselves shaping our behavior.

2. There are three excellent books that deal with childhood and adolescence and our cultural dilemma: David Elkind, *All Grown Up and No Place to Go: Teenagers in Crisis* (Reading, Mass.: Addison-Wesley, 1984); idem, *The Hurried Child: Growing Up Too Fast Too Soon* (Reading, Mass.: Addison-Wesley, 1981); and Neil Postman, *The Disappearance of Childhood* (New York: Dell Books, 1984).

### Chapter 5

1. I have discussed the foundations of these issues in *Bonding*, see esp. chap. 8, "Adolescence: Is There Life after Puberty?"

2. Compare cross-cultural measures in stages of moral reasoning. An early report is found in Lawrence Kohlberg's "The Child as a Moral Philosopher." Additional documentation in the cross-cultural measurement of this Harvard-based research effort was reported by Elliot Turiel and others in *The Philosophy of Moral Development*, ed. Lawrence Kohlberg et al., 2 vols. (New York: Harper & Row, 1981).

3. See the phenomenon that baffled researchers Robert Coles and Geoffrey Stokes in their report on a *Rolling Stone* survey in *Sex and the American Teenager*. Stokes reports, e.g., that some kids who are planning to enter sexual relationships want to be told by their parents to wait.

"Be careful" is not at all the subject they have in mind; they crave having tools for making the judgment about how soon to be sexually intimate. Note also Coles's analysis of the survey in his closing chapter, "Reconsiderations," 195ff.

4. See *Re-Bonding;* virtually the entire book is devoted to identifying and dealing with the pain of sexual experience.

## Chapter 6

1. See Urie Bronfenbrenner, "Report of Forum 15—Children and Parents: Together in the World," in *Report to the President: White House Conference on Children* (Washington, D.C.: Government Printing Office, 1970). For further treatment of the same issues, see Bronfenbrenner's book, *The Two Worlds of Childhood: USA and USSR* (New York: Simon & Schuster, 1972), esp. the chapter entitled "The Unmaking of the American Child."

2. Reported by Bronfenbrenner in "The Disturbing Changes in the American Family," *Search* (Fall 1976): 4ff. He cites U.S. Census Bureau statistics on the changing number of adults in the average household.

3. This excerpt from the 30 August 1976 issue of *The New Yorker* appeared as the back cover feature in *Search* (Fall 1976).

## Chapter 7

1. H. Stephen Glenn summarizes many of these issues in his workshops for professionals who work with drug addiction. You can get these lectures in his audio tape series, *Developing Capable Young People* and *Principles of Personal Power and Influence.* Both are available direct from him at Box 318, Lexington, S.C. Glenn interprets what is now being called family systems research and theory. I became aware of this perspective long before the systemic reality was observed. It appears in the discussion of satellization in the growing child as described in David Ausubel, *Theory and Problems of Adolescent Development* (New York: Grune & Stratton, 1954). A similar perspective identifying family conditions from which to predict delinquency or nondelinquency had emerged in Sheldon Glueck and Eleanor Glueck, *Unraveling Juvenile Delinquency* (Cambridge, Mass.: Harvard University Press, 1950). Robert Sears and Lucy Rau also reported on aspects of family systems in their *Patterns in Child Rearing* (Stanford, Calif.: Stanford University Press, 1957) and *Identification and Child Rearing* (Stanford, Calif.: Stanford University Press, 1965).

2. See *Bonding,* esp. 136ff, concerning father absence, mother deprivation, and predictable problems.

3. See Peter Druck, *The Secrets Men Keep: Breaking the Silence Barrier* (Garden City, N.Y.: Doubleday and Co., 1985).

4. Kenneth Hamilton and Alice Hamilton, *To Be a Man—To Be a Woman* (Nashville: Abingdon, 1975), 19.

5. See *Bonding,* 156ff.

## Chapter 8

1. See Salvador Minuchin, *Family Kaleidoscope* (Cambridge, Mass.: Harvard University Press, 1984).

2. For a fascinating summary of a large number of the aspects of systemic reality, see Charles Hampden-Turner, *Maps of the Mind* (New York: Macmillan, 1981). Map 25, "The Holographic Mind: Karl Pribriam," reports how Pribriam at Stanford University used the systemic theory generated by Dennis Gabor's pioneering work on the hologram.

3. See my proposal for a systemic theology put forward in "The Contemporary Church as 'Holy Community': Call to Corporate Character and Life," in *The Church: An Inquiry into Ecclesiology from a Biblical Theological Perspective*, ed. Melvin E. Dieter and Daniel N. Berg (Anderson, Ind.: Warner Press, 1984).

4. W. Robert Beavers, "The Application of Family Systems Theory to Crisis Intervention," in *The Minister as Crisis Counselor*, ed. David Switzer (Nashville: Abingdon, 1974). Beavers uses technical psychiatric language to describe the various systems. What I have called here the competitive system he likely would call the behavior-disordered family.

5. My first empirical research took shape as my dissertation, "Value-Oriented Instruction in the Church and in the Home," Ph.D. diss., Indiana University, 1969. Two recent enthnographic projects have been published in my agency newsletter, *Catalyst*. They are each reported in a series of four installments: "Seasons of a Pastor's Life" (1984– 85) and "What Postpones Intimacy until Marriage" (1986–87). See also endnote 1 for chapter 7 for citations of other systems studies.

6. Sheldon Glueck and Eleanor Glueck, *Unraveling Juvenile Delinquency* (Cambridge, Mass.: Harvard University Press, 1950).

7. Nick Stinnett and John DeFrain, *Secrets of Strong Families* (New York: Little, Brown, and Co., 1985). These University of Nebraska researchers were frustrated with studies about what is wrong with families, so they went in search of healthy families, locating their first sample of three thousand through home demonstration agents and county agents. Today some thirty thousand families have been surveyed. The six strengths they found universal among what they call strong families are reported in chapter 10.

8. See *Lovers.*

9. Nick Stinnett and John DeFrain, *The Secrets of Strong Families* (New York: Little, Brown, and Co., 1986), 114–15.

10. See ibid., 14, for a summary of the findings. I recommend the paperback Berkeley edition of their book.

11. Ibid.

## Chapter 9

1. See James Michael Lee's summary of these sensitive periods for value change in his chapter, "Some Key Findings about Learning," in *The Flow of Religious Instruction* (Birmingham: Religious Education Press, 1973), esp. 106ff.

## Chapter 10

1. Brooke Hayward, *Haywire* (New York: Bantam, 1978), 367–68.

2. Sheldon Glueck and Eleanor Glueck, *Unraveling Juvenile Delinquency* (Cambridge, Mass.: Harvard University Press, 1950).

## Chapter 11

1. See W. Robert Beavers, "The Application of Family Systems Theory to Crisis Intervention," in *The Minister as Crisis Counselor*, ed. David Switzer (Nashville: Abingdon, 1974). His findings are roughly equivalent to my four categories:

Competitive = Behaviorally Disordered
Chaotic = Disturbed
Showcase = Neurotic
Intimate = Healthy

Beavers arranges his systems into three types as follows (pp. 184–85):

1. Seriously disturbed—most entropic
   a. family is queer, odd, strange
   b. lack of individual boundaries
   c. strong sense of timelessness
   d. poor parental coalition; a child often powerful
   e. frequent speaking for others
   f. unresponsive to one another
   g. individual choice impossible
   h. poor task performance
2. Midrange—rigidly structured
   a. autonomy possible, but severely restricted
   b. people's essential nature seen as evil
   c. child-rearing seen as battle for control
   d. ubiquitous referee dominates family members
   e. parental coalition either poor or good by subjugation of one parent
   f. feeling tone varies from polite to angry or depressed
   g. scapegoating frequent
   h. resistant to change but hope for good change is alive
3. Healthy—structure with flexibility
   a. high degree of autonomy
   b. people's essential nature seen as neutral or good
   c. feeling tone positive, frequent laughter
   d. frequent real encounters, sharing
   e. extremely open and receptive
   f. good parental coalition
   g. power shared, no domination
   h. high task efficiency

You can see from scanning Beavers's summary that my chaotic and showcase families are formed out of parts of systems 1 and 2 above. I am influenced strongly by H. Stephen Glenn and by the Glueck findings on family cohesiveness, as well as by systems management theory in which corresponding interpersonal relationships tend to appear. See E. Mansell Pattison, *Pastor and Parish: A Systems Approach* (Philadelphia: Fortress Press, 1977).

2. See the Fonzie syndrome material in *Bonding*, 137ff.

3. See the Aldonza pattern discussed in ibid., 141ff.

4. Beavers describes the showcase family as the neurotic family. Their tendency toward tranquilizers, amphetamines, and sleeping medications are cited in his "Application of Family Systems Theory," 203.

5. For a closer look at the ways we tend to misunderstand teachings about submission, authority, and dominion, see *Lovers*. The book is based on the premise that relationships determine roles, and not the other way round.

6. Check the Lifestyle features of popular newspapers for regular articles illustrating this contradiction. One particularly biting feature was written by Richard Phillips and Janet Franz of the Knight-Ridder News Service. I saw it as it appeared in the Springfield, Ohio, *News-Sun*, 11 April 1987, under the title, "The Great Debate: Are Men Really Jerks?"

7. See "Chain of Command: The Naturalistic Fallacy Goes to Church!" in *Lovers*, 81ff.

8. In *Lovers*, Robbie's story is told as a three-layered unfolding. We also treat her story as a dialogue when we use it in a seminar setting. We call our journey "The Seasons of Marriage." We were at first surprised that both men and women responded to it saying that they felt somehow freed from the curses and consequences of the traditional Fall-based relationship (which is so popular in all cultures).

9. I called that lecture "Creation, Adam, and Woman"; see *Lovers*, 22ff., and *Bonding*, 21ff.

### Chapter 12

1. See Hugo Lagercrantz and Theodore Slotkin, "Stress of Being Born," *Scientific American* 254 (April 1986): 100ff. They report that vaginally delivered babies arrive with a natural high and an alertness that is prompted by the brain's release of chemicals triggered by the stress of passing through the birth canal. They tend to remain alert and sensitized to their environments for a few hours. It is during this endorphin high that birth bonding tends to occur. This may be an explanation for why we have certain bonded memories related to stress situations. An earlier and useful discussion on birth bonding is Hara Estroff Marano's "Biology Is One Key to the Bonding of Mothers and Babies," *Smithsonian* 11 (February 1981): 60ff.

2. See *Bonding*, 3.

3. Sheldon Vanauken, *A Severe Mercy* (New York: Harper & Row, 1977), 37, 212–13.

4. See *Bonding*, 108ff.

5. Robert Coles's chapter ("A Domain of Sorts") is in *Humanscape: Environments for People*, ed. Stephen Kaplan and Rachel Kaplan (North Scituate, Mass.: Duxbury Press, 1978), 91ff.

6. See *Bonding*, 33–62.

7. For a further discussion of promiscuity as fornication and as sexual addiction, see *Re-Bonding*.

8. Robert Coles, "Names Written in the Bible," in *Humanscape*, ed. Kaplan and Kaplan, 341ff.

## Chapter 13

1. John Westerhoff, *Will Our Children Have Faith?* (New York: Seabury Press, 1976). Walter Brueggemann responded to both this title and Westerhoff's understanding of the nature of our problem in his inaugural address as he was installed on 10 February 1983 in the Evangelical Chair of Biblical Interpretation at Eden Theological Seminary in St. Louis. This address, later published, was entitled "Will Our Faith Have Children?" Westerhoff obviously puts the pressure on us, as if by working harder we could guarantee faith to our children. Brueggeman focuses on the quality of our faith, suggesting that it has an existence of its own and that its fertility and reproductive ability have more to do with the quality of our faith than with how clever we are in our educational and evangelism techniques.

2. More than thirty years ago, during the summer of 1957, I did workshops at four locations in the precentennial convocations of the Free Methodist Church. During these I quoted what must have been a line made indelible to me by W. Dale Cryderman who had returned from a stint in Japan with Youth for Christ. I am quite sure he is the first person I heard use the phrase, "God has no grandchildren." The point is clear if we take the evangelical sense in which we respond personally to God's grace in the new birth. Indeed such a proposition stands in stark contrast to birthright traditions and to the Jewish tradition of the nature of faith communities.

3. "Doing faith" is a concept that James W. Fowler defines and illustrates in his *Stages of Faith* (San Francisco: Harper & Row, 1981).

4. Carol Gilligan found that women are uniquely able to organize the moral universe around issues related to attachment. See her "In a Different Voice: Women's Conceptions of Self and Morality," *Harvard Educational Review* 47 (1977): 492– 505.

5. Jean Piaget ("Cooperation and the Idea of Justice," in *The Moral Judgment of the Child*) and Lawrence Kohlberg (in his 1958 dissertation at the University of Chicago) identified justice as the core of morality. Kohlberg's best statement is found in "Stages of Moral Development as a Basis for Moral Education," in *Moral Education*, ed. Clive Beck et al. (Toronto: University of Toronto Press, 1970).

6. See my discussion of attachment and justice in Donald M. Joy, *Moral Development Foundations: Judeo-Christian Alternatives to Piaget/Kohlberg* (Nashville: Abingdon, 1983), 13ff.

7. We discuss this issue from many sides in *Lovers*.

# Index

△

# Scripture Index